ROPE

ROPE

MARIE KETSIA THEODORE-PHAREL

Nou La Nonprofit LLC

To all unseen cocottes.

"We learn the rope of life by untying its knots" – Jean Toomer, *Definitions and Aphorisms, Ll, 1931*

Prologue

A line of blood spread under Colvin's blackened nail. The one he'd been scraping with his knife. He was sprawled on his belly—hidden by brush and a large moss-covered boulder, looking down at the dark little bodies below. They seemed like small dolls hurrying through the ravine, heading—no doubt—toward the village marketplace. Everybody was passing along the side of the mountain, down through the ravine, headed away from the forest and toward the bustling village just outside of the northern metropolis of Okap. Why didn't I pick Port-au-Prince or Leogane like the other trackers? Colvin chastised himself. He ran his hand through his brittle, unwashed, three-month-old beard.

Suddenly his boredom was arrested and cuffed to the image of a woman on a mule approaching the forest. The forest that had hidden from him the one thing he needed to be free. As he watched the woman, the pages of his Bible which rested a few inches from his left elbow, fluttered. There was no wind. Is this an omen, he wondered? Then Colvin reasoned: women go to the market to sell. The marketplace is in the opposite direction. What would a woman be doing heading for the forest? He had heard that not even the voodoo priests or the most powerful masons go in there.

Slowly, he crawled from behind the moss-covered rock and brush where he had been watching the travelers. He grabbed the reins of his mule and found a place to hide his steed. The woman and her donkey hadn't been going fast. He followed her on foot for about half a mile into the forest, but when she reached a canopy of trees, she vanished. One minute she was in front of him, and the next he saw a bird fly away and she was gone.

Colvin kicked the underbrush and cursed. Finally in exhaustion, he let himself collapse to the floor. Suddenly he had a hunch—something he and his fellow tracking team hadn't considered. How had the rebels been able to survive and evade trackers for so long? They had female counter parts! No one would suspect a woman, he reasoned. *And these Haitian bitches play the part well.* He was seething now. *Well, she's gotta come out of the forest. So, I'll wait for her.* He created a nest for himself under that canopy of trees where the woman disappeared and waited.

Three days later, the woman emerged from the darker inner forest to where he nested. Colvin noticed immediately that there was nothing on the mule. All the sacks she'd had on the mule when she went into the deep forest, which he imagined to be the likes of breadfruit flour, cured meats, and medicine were gone. As she neared where he laid camouflaged by plants and moss, he slashed her mule across its knees. It brayed and threw the woman off. She fell and bumped her head. The mule clambered toward the ravine that led to the village.

The woman was on her back. He placed his gutting knife under her nose. Light mists told him she was alive, but she was not moving. He noted her well-proportioned face, but also that the darkened circles under her eyes detracted from her beauty—if this kind of a person can be considered beautiful, he told himself. Again, not wanting any surprises, he waved his hands slowly above her nose and confirmed that she was not pretending and that she was still breathing and unconscious. He tied her hands above her head. As she laid unconscious, he made a fire, for the morning sun had receded under the threat of clouds. He placed a couple of dried logs on the fire. Ambers and sparks flew around like fireflies. Then he straddled, intending to wake her. Her eyes grew wide as she attempted to free herself. He felt how soft she was under him. He hadn't felt that softness in almost two years. Her movement triggered visions of soft white thighs from his Regular at the brothel back home. He ripped open her shirt. He told himself he wanted to make sure that she was indeed a female. Her breast spilled out onto his hands. His hands worked fast at releasing himself from his pants. Even as she bit into his callous palm in protest, he didn't stop.

A little later, he lifted his sweaty forehead from the crook of her shoulder where it had been resting. He looked into her eyes and saw the tears. He told himself this was a ploy to weaken him. After all, she'd put a spell on him. Why else would he touch a nigger woman? He had never even thought of such a thing before. "I'm going to untie your hands, don't do anything stupid. As he untied her hands, he asked, what do they call you?" She said her name so softly, he almost missed it: "Poupette". He laughed at the silliness of the name. That woman was the furthest thing from the pink-cheeked dolls the name evoked and which his sisters had played with when they were children. The thought of his sisters took him off guard. He thought of his family, something he never allowed himself to do. He remembered their bodies spread across the train track. He remembered the American Natives who didn't ask for that train to come through their land, picking up the pieces of his family.

Suddenly, his body was pierced by the pain of Poupette's knife lodged into his shoulder. With the speed of a lion on his prey, he punched her across the face and she fell back. He tied her down again. After, he wrapped a tourniquet around his shoulder to stop the bleeding. Then he started to beat Poupette on the soles of her feet. "Did you bring those supplies to the Cacos? How many other female guerrillas are there? Where is Champagne hiding? How many are hiding with him?" The questions ran from him like the rivulet of sweat that dripped down his chest. He hung her by her tied hands from a strong branch. Then he built a fire under her. She only moaned. Words that he didn't understand came out of her mouth, like she was speaking an ancient language, casting a spell he thought.

When she finally addressed him, the sun was setting. "You've had your run, but as soon as night comes, I will turn into a wolf and tear you to pieces."

"Is that so?" Colvin said. He thought of how she had disappeared from in front of him and all he had seen was a bird flying away. If you don't believe in voodoo, it can't hurt you, he told himself. Still, something about her calmness and resilience scared him. He climbed up the tree and cut her down. She screamed as she landed on the hard floor. Colvin straddled her neck and held her held down with his forearm. He forced her mouth open and stuff leaves in it. He tied her mouth. Then, holding her down, he carved a cross on her nose. "This is what we do to witches and werewolves where I come from."

Six months later...

Blood seeped out of the black man's ankle. Colvin's blue eyes flitted from the screaming man to the flutters in the branches above. He had prayed for this day, but somehow he imagined there would be more sun light when he captured this man. If the sun were high, he would be sure of his footsteps, but with only dim light penetrating the deep green canopy of the forest, he knew he had to be very careful as he moved about.

"Champagne, stop pulling the rope, you're making it worse," Colvin snapped, taking careful steps not to trigger another trap.

A guttural, "So, you know my name?" came out of Champagne. Colvin continued to move to the spelling of the letters of Mount Vernon and ignored Champagne's light taunt. "Lying here bleeding in your trap is not an accident." Champagne cobbled the sentences in between gasps and deep breaths. "I'm your prey." Beads of sweat dripped from his neatly shaped moustache and hit his protruding cleft bones. "Well, I wasn't one hundred percent, but you just confirmed it," Colvin laughed at Champagne's sharp intake of breath.

Colvin squatted in front of him. *In five hours this man is going to be dead.* Colvin repeated that sentence in his head and each time it meant something different. The first time Colvin thought about the few hours that stood between him and his place in history the idea made him feel light—like at any moment he was going to float away. Maybe there'll be a page about him in every history book. He pictured beautiful, cherry-cheeked, blonde, blue-eyed—true American kids—reading about him. Will they place him next to his hero, George Washington? The thought of his picture, his name, and his heroics being placed on the same page as George Washington made his heart race and the feeling of lightness returned.

"FUCKING AMERICANS!" Champagne shouted, his pitch reverberant, announcing, and informing the forest.

"Stop screaming and I'll remove the trap. You have to be really still," Colvin warned, but the thought that this ordeal was going to be over in a few hours popped in his head again, and he almost said it out loud as he ran his rough hands through his long, matted beard, delighting in the fact that he had indeed captured the elusive man—a rebel. Colvin wondered how his superiors would receive him. Colonel Rheich, with a mouth full of chewing tobacco, would say, "Donner, you dumb sonnamabeach, you did it. Made history like those crazy 'cesters of yorn on da Oregon trail. I knowed you had it in you. Good blud that one!"

Colvin also pictured himself riding into the makeshift garrison of Fort Dimanche with the injured man tied up. Would all the other soldiers who hadn't been able to do it clap for him, pat him on the back?

He looked at Champagne's face again. Colvin smiled as his captive shook his head from left to right. He wanted to say something about Champagne's well-maintained moustache, but instead a wide smile formed on Colvin's lips. This was the thing people loved about Champagne—an extraordinary gentleman even during a war. Colvin wasn't surprised to see that what he had heard of the legendary Caco, as his rebel group was called, was actually true. Few legends lived up to stories. He thought about telling Champagne that, but changed his mind. *It might give him the idea that I like him.* Instead, Colvin said, "Six months, you piece of shit. I've been cooped up in a hole for six months trying to catch you. Yes, I'm the hunter and you're the prey. You a slippery mother fucker."

Champagne closed his eyes, and Colvin wondered if he was fighting that sensation of the soul wanting to leave the body. Colvin pulled on the rope around his captive's torso and Champagne's eyes jolted open; they were like full moons rattling in his head. The pain contorted his body, making an instrument out of him. Colvin laughed, "You know, when we couldn't find you about nine months ago, we, in the tracking team, split up. Everybody thought you were in Port-au-Prince or Leogane. Some of the guys were fighting for that. I said no, I bet he'll go where no one expects. I ask for the deep forest of the North Country. Everybody laughed. Colvin you dumb son of a bitch they laughed. Well, hee hee hee. Look who's laughing now." He paused for a minute and saw that Champagne's eyes were open and Colvin felt encouraged that Champagne seemed vaguely interested in his story.

Colvin reached into one of the numerous pockets sewn into his green camouflage jacket. He retrieved a small flask. "Drink this so that the poison on the trap won't build up in your veins." Champagne turned his face away. "Drink it--it's not American made. I promise. You'll never believe how I found you. Female guerrillas. That was really clever." He licked his lip and in a very suggestive manner said, "I had me a little bit of a Poupette."

Champagne shot up despite the rope cutting into him. He screamed. If sounds were blades, his would have cut Colvin into small bits. Champagne collapsed to the floor, doubling and wincing.

Colvin waited for him to calm down. He approached with the drink again. "Seriously, have this. It will help with the pain." When Champagne made no move to open his mouth, Colvin continued, "Your own people made it. Just like this trap—best Haitian iron work. Don't it just eat at you?" Colvin cackled, hitting the meaty part of Champagne's thigh. His laughter boomeranged against the dense foliage. "Here you are thinking that you're this big time hero of Haiti and the crafts designed by your own people are killing you?" Colvin laughed uncontrollably, holding the sides of his stomach. He moved closer, facing Champagne who was panting. Birds swooped from branches as Colvin's laughter reverberated. Champagne pulled at the rope. Colvin sniggered, "Haven't you realized that the more you pull, the tighter the trap around your ankle gets?" Then, he kneeled on one knee to remove Champagne's hands from the rope wound tightly around his bare chest. Colvin pinched Champagne's nose as he placed the flask to his lips, pulling down on his chin until Champagne swallowed enough of the antidote.

"My life is my own," Champagne spouted between labored breaths and forced gulps.

"Oh really. Enlighten me—you're caught in my trap, so your life is in my hands--" Colvin broke his sentence midway as a flash of blue disappeared into the verdant canopy. "You better send a signal to whoever's up there. Make them go away or I will kill them and you right here. Trust me—your next best move is for me to take you to Port-au-Prince alive where my superiors will let you make a last statement before dying," Colvin said, hoping Champagne will buy his bluff. The truth is, he didn't know why his superiors demanded that anyone who captured Champagne not kill him. When Champagne made no move, Colvin continued, "Trust me. They will kill you, but you can make a statement to stop this insanity. You can prevent more of your people from being killed."

Champagne closed his eyes, a sign Colvin took as the medicine was already taking its effect. Champagne slurred, "People often don't understand that the life they seek to destroy can become the line that tows them in."

"Spare me the metaphors. Did you spout metaphors for the twenty U.S. naval officers you killed?"

"You waged war on us and killed us a thousand times over. Every morning, every street in Port-au-Prince and Okap, you leave dead bodies on our streets."

"What is it you people like to say, Haiti--the first independent black nation since 1804? If you hadn't been a mess, we wouldn't have had to invade."

Champagne coughed and Colvin squeezed Champagne's nose, taking the opportunity of his open mouth to drop more of the antidote in. Champagne spat, "I don't know why you bother. At any moment, I can leave this body if I want to. You see over there--" Champagne pointed two fingers towards the horizon to the only patch of sky, a blue hole among the thick green forest. "Standing there is a long line of warriors. Shango and Ogun united."

At that moment there was a flash of lightning followed by drumming thunder that seized the forest. Colvin wiped his eyes with the back of his hand because for a minute he thought he saw the rope at his feet vibrate, recoil after the flash of lightning. "Oh, there it is. I was waiting for the hocus pocus voodoo nonsense. It was just a coincidence that lightning and thunder happened when you said that."

"My ancestors –warrior spirits are waiting for me. I can leap out of my body like warriors before me did. Warriors like Boukman, Makandal, and Dessalines to name a few. Leading them right there is Shango. Don't you see his towering size beyond that tree? Allow me to let you feel the banging of their swords and shields!" Champagne lifted his hands and a bolt of lightning came through and hit a nearby tree. A thud and yelp resounded through the forest.

Colvin wouldn't admit it if someone were beating it out of him, but for one minute he saw in the trees hundreds of warriors. Were they actual living followers of the rebel coming to free him or were they, as Champagne insisted, a guardian force of warrior ancestors? Colvin shook his head, chastising himself for entertaining that last thought.

Champagne lifted his hand and another bolt electrified the air.

"Do you want me to keep going?" Champagne smirked, a sign Colvin interpreted as amusement and acknowledgement that Champagne knew by the unnerved look on Colvin's face that he was somewhat scared. Colvin breathe in, puffing his chest he said, "Suit yourself, but no lightning god is gonna take you alive from me. You'll die in less than five hours—just enough time to get you to Port-au-Prince and turn you in," Colvin said as he cocked his pistol, "but your death can be sooner if you don't tell your men to back off. I saw them when lightning hit the trees."

"They are not men like you and me. They are the ancestral warriors."

"Okay, suit yourself." Colvin began to shoot toward the trees. After several shots, he stopped to gauge Champagne's reaction.

Champagne's eyes were still closed as he said, "I'm only staying here for you. You have crossed our fates. The very rope with which you bind me will anchor our destinies."

"Blah, blah, blah," Colvin said as he removed Champagne's ankle from the metal trap. He poured some of the coagulating powder over the wound. Champagne sucked in his breath. Colvin placed his knee on the good ankle—just in case Champagne had ideas about kicking him or escaping. He wrapped the wounded foot and then with his rope, Colvin tied Champagne as if he were a mummy. Colvin placed him over the horse and climbed on behind him.

A few miles later, Colvin thought he heard something—as if someone was tracking him. He was almost at the mouth of the forest. He saw the spot where he had watched the village and the spot where he had first spotted Poupette. Then, for a fleeting moment, he saw a row of about twenty female guerrillas on the other side of the gulley. He could see from the ones who stood side ways that the women had their cutlass strapped to their back and shotguns to the front. They wore green headscarves like Poupette and that told him, but they were unmistakably soldiers. He cocked his pistol and placed it on Champagne's head. He knew if they could take him, they would have already done it a few miles back when they started tracking him. Then, just as they had appeared, they disappeared into the brush. He propelled his horse forward.

A few hundred yards from edge of the forest, he passed a mound where a placard with a badly scribbled name identified the dead. He couldn't tell if it was Take Cosmos or Jake Cosmos. The only word that was clear was *American*. Colvin couldn't help but feel blessed that he was making it out alive. Nevertheless, he couldn't get rid of the nagging feeling that this American was buried in an area where he himself had buried a lot of explosives. Had his brethren fallen by his hand? Should he remove the explosives he'd buried? There was no time, he told himself. In four hours, I will have my medal for capturing the most dangerous man to the American government--- Champagne Pepla, one of the leaders of the infamous Cacos.

Moiselle ripped the ring from her necklace and tossed it down the well. She was sorry she could not hurl herself down there as well. The small jade ring didn't make big ripples; it barely disturbed her reflection. She pursed her dark plum lips and closed her eyes, visualizing the green ring as it sat at the bottom of where it might stay for an eternity. She picked up the ladle. It jingled as it hit the side of the well's rusted lid. She bent her head and touched her tongue to the cool water.

The call of a vulture flying above compelled her to look up. "Lend me your eyes, *malfini*," she said to the bird. The bad-news bird complied; now Moiselle was soaring in the air above the rows of thatched roof houses. She compelled her bird-eyes to go beyond the big tall trees.

See, there are the houses she wanted to live in. There was the largest one. Set apart. A sprawling stone home with marbled lions guarding a tall red gate. She had stumbled upon that estate once while roaming the woods, but she was never able to find it again. It impressed her greatly that someone had the ability to hide a big house like that in plain sight. What kind of thing could do this magic? Sadly, she thought, money. *Bad-news bird, help me see that house again.* She held the ladle the way she'd seen the woman on the balcony hold a glass with wine, and she was swishing the well water when she heard a deep voice say, "You must love water."

She didn't move. She knew by his inflection and accent that he was a white man.

"That water for drinking, Miss?"

She twisted around and wiped her wet hands on the front of her house dress. The speaker, suddenly present like a tree you missed until you needed shelter, swung a rope from hand to hand nonchalantly as he awaited her answer. She saw another rope—the one in her dream where a mermaid with wings is tied to a tree. Her mother said never to repeat that dream. It was a bad sign from the goddess, Ezili. She scanned the stranger from his weathered cowboy boots and jeans to his white shirt cuffed at the elbows. Out of habit, she backed away from him.

"Are you a soldier? What are you doing here? This is private property," she stammered, but then upon a second, closer look at his ashen knuckles, wet curly blond hair and cowboy hat held by short straps around his neck, she suspected it was not a smart question. She admonished herself for asking the kind of question likely to come out of her father's mouth. She had an overwhelming urge to reach out and uncoil one of those twisted blond curls, but she should probably be scared of a stranger, her inner voice reminded her. Trying not to show apprehension, she ran her long, thin fingers through her hair, grateful she had hot-combed it and had taken her chignon down from earlier. The light wind blew it around her face.

The man's muscles flexed as he pointed in the direction he came from. "Sorry to be on your property, I was just looking for my dog," he said. She raised an eyebrow, and said, "You didn't answer my question."

He smiled and said, "No, I'm not," he said. "I'm guessing there haven't been soldiers around here for over a decade."

"My pa..." She rephrased what she was going to say. "Some people think that the Americans haven't left. That they are here undercover pretending to be missionaries, reporters, and researchers." The young man scoffed and then mumbled, "The occupation has been over for more than a decade now". Moiselle rolled her eyes, daring him to get into an argument with her. She knew she could win. She would tell him story after story about the secret soldiers stashed in broad daylight, living among them and still trying to run Haiti just as her father ranted in the past. But the stranger simply shook his head as he repeated the word "soldier". Then he pointed to the ladle, "May I have a drink please?" Despite the fact that she was being pulled into the deep greenness of his eyes, calling to her like the ring at the bottom of the well, "My water is not for charity," she said.

From a distance, she heard her father yell, "Moiselle, who is that you're talking with?" Her father was in the blue barn where the animals slept. She knew he could reach the well in ten of his long strides if she needed him. "If it's one of those undercover American soldiers, tell him we have nothing for him and this *volesanzave* needs to keep moving right out of Haiti. Those thieves can fall into the sea as far as I'm concerned."

"There's no one here, Papa," she said as the white man ducked behind a tree, putting his finger to his lips. Her father's voice cut welts on her back, like the ones she'd received the day before at his hands. She looked at the white man's rope, cringing at the thought of what her father could do to her with it.

Nevertheless, Moiselle did like the way her father's voice exuded authority, making the foreigner's throat constrict and his Adam's apple move up and down, slowly. Out of habit she touched her necklace, looking for the ring that used to hang and nestle under her shirt in between her breasts. Then she remembered the sound it made as it plummeted into the silence of that cold water. Once the rhythmic hammering of her father resumed, the stranger moved from behind the tree and approached her. She handed him the ladle of water. He drank and slowly and washed his face with a second scoop. After he was done, Moiselle said, "Well, are you going to pay or not?"

"For what?"

"The water. What else?" Moiselle said. As his eyes grew, she continued, "No matter what you think you've heard about us country girls, we don't sell that. If that's what you're looking for, you'll have better luck in Port-au-Prince."

"Miss," the stranger scoffed, "that was the farthest thing from my mind. I mean...I don't mean to say that I am not interested," he stopped and stomped his foot, rubbing his gloved hand through the tufts of blond curls. "Okay, let's start over. I'm Robert. And I meant no disrespect."

"I'm Moiselle," she said.

"Me wings in Kreyol. Or is it short for Mademoiselle?" He asked. She shrugged. He continued, "Either way, it's pretty and different. Suddenly she didn't know what to do with her hands that he had shaken, or how to take the compliment. They stared at each other. He wasn't much taller than her. When they went to say something, his words covered hers.

"Well, speaking of wings. I heard for tomorrow's New Year celebration, 19 bombers and then 45 fighter planes might be flying above," Robert said.

Moiselle wondered why he had such a wide grin and proud look about such a frightening event. "Why are they going to be flying above? Is it another invasion?"

He laughed and shook his head. "No, it's just to put on a show."

"Oh, I get it. 1945," Moiselle said, scraping her feet in the dirt.

Robert pointed eastward, over her head, "You know what, I'm staying over yonder. I've been setting up the tent for the month long revival that starts tomorrow. I'll tell you what--give me some more of that water and I'll invite you to our revival. I'll share a different kind of water with you--you'll never be thirsty again."

Shadows of various shapes filtered through the nearby mango tree and painted his arms. His side profile jarred her memory; she now remembered where she had seen him. Indeed, he had been hammering something in the ground that morning as she rode on her parents' mule, accompanying her mother to the market—an escape from her father while he calmed down.

"Will there be anise tea and fresh bread like they give at the missionary school?" Moiselle asked.

"No, it's not a social. We'll have a lot of singing and bringing the Holy Spirit down here to save some souls." Moiselle's brows furrowed and she caught herself before asking, how can they be lost when they are here? She brushed off his statement as weird things foreigners say.

"Well, you're not going to have a lot of people come unless you offer refreshments," Moiselle instructed. Just then Moiselle spotted her mother and the mules about three hundred feet away. The animal was still loaded down with burgundy colored sugar cane stalks, green pumpkins, and brown yams, but it looked lighter than it had that morning when they left for market. She had already spent too much time speaking to this white man. She envisioned her mother clenching her teeth, pursing her lips tightly. So, despite her apprehension, she handed Robert the ladle of water. He took a sip and then winked at her.

"Come tomorrow to taste some real water. Ask for me, Robert Donner, and I will take care of you. I'll save you a special seat."

She watched his broad back as he walked towards her mother. Her brother and sister took turns with a slingshot trying to shoot birds at nearby trees. At the point where Robert and her mother met, he took his hat off to her; her mother stopped the beast. Moiselle imagined her saying her salutations. But it was the look on Robert's face that perplexed her. Had he met her mother before? Did he recognize someone else in her mother's face? Now she would definitely have to go to his revival to ask him.

Moiselle looked around as if it were her last day on this earth, in this country, in this town, or on this farm. In the distance, the smoke from the State's sugar cane factory tricked the clouds to approach and then dirtied them. Imposing palm fronds loomed above encroaching flat green banana trees. At the post with the compound's name, Promised Land, scribbled on it, Moiselle looked back at the one-room mud houses, sheltered by the tallest *siwel* trees, lined up in rows as stiff as children undergoing a catechism lesson. They reminded her of her few inconsistent years in missionary school to learn religion, not reading. She could recite the few verses she had learned, but she could not read any letters. She shuddered at the thought of dying in this town before she saw any other place.

She would not miss that light brown earth constantly sliding or shifting after a minor sprinkle.

Moiselle's palms itched. This was a sign she was going to get money. She touched the taut leaves of the few remaining pumpkins and sprouts in the patch to take away the itch. Those were the few her mother was saving for tomorrow's New Year's soup. The tomatoes were already too tall for the small stakes that were supposed to be holding them.

She saw the life that her father envisioned for her, which included marriage to Jean Samson. He was part of her father's late night conspiracy talks. Samson's father had a sweet potato farm, which made Samson the best prospect. She didn't want to imagine herself with him. She only had another year at best to change her future, she reasoned. After that, the pressure to marry Jean Samson would not only come from her father's flogging, but he would probably drag her to the church. Jean Samson was so very plain; he didn't walk around with a rope around his shoulder, she thought.

She thought about all the color and vibrancy that were in the plants. *I want to be alive like that.* She loved the *rara* songs and dances. This was why, despite lashings from her father's leather whips, when the ragtag raras came to town, she trailed these impromptu bands of musicians with home-honed instruments—cyclical metals that clanged, spiky metal that grated, roared, or echoed deranged laughter. She abandoned housework and ran after the rara band, followed in a dancing frenzy, a spirit-filled-body dance, gyrating as to unscrew all sadness out of her life, dancing all the way to Saut D'eau or Thomazeau.

She walked to the top of her family's property, counting fifty posts until she met her mother.

"Did you do the wash and fetch water to fill the pots yet?" Moiselle's mother asked when Moiselle met her at the farm's entrance. She took the reins of one of the donkeys, helped her younger siblings off, and started to unload her mother's donkey. "Manman, that blan said there's the miracle revival starting tomorrow, can I go this year?"

"Why is it that every white man coming to this country finds you? And I have to hear from the neighbors, 'Mrs. Moise, did you know your daughter was talking to this white man or that American?' You are only fifteen, girl. Why can't you wait until you're grown to live? You want to do all your living in one day--in one breath." The wind carried her mother's words away as Moiselle took the donkeys to the stable.

****

Earlier that morning, while nailing an anchor, Robert had looked up to see a beautiful girlish woman who sat regally astride a donkey, her shoulders and midriff moving rhythmically back and forth. He stared at her. When she passed, her lids didn't flutter. He imagined her saying hello to him, and he, telling her how the hibiscus flower tucked into her chignon made her look beautiful.

"You don't want to get involved with her, brother," Jean Pierre said, watching the way Robert stared. "She is complicated."

"I was looking at the donkey. Have you finished painting the benches?" Robert asked, waving away the smell of turpentine that oozed out of Jean Pierre, while trying to hide his irritation. At that moment, all he wanted to do was chase the girl on that donkey.

"Young Pastor, you turn red when you lie. I told you—say the word and I'll take you to see some real sweet ladies. I'm talking about cinnamon-colored, sweet-talking girls—not complicated girls like that one."

"Complicated? That's a big word for an *ougan*," Robert said, as he faked throwing jabs at Jean Pierre.

"Correction, Little Pastor, I'm a healer and musician."

"For the life of me, I don't know why you've come to two revivals yet you refuse to convert. Do you come for the free food?"

"That hurts," Jean Pierre said, feigning injury. "Little Pastor, I love a good party and a sweet woman, and I'm telling you for your own good," he paused and spat on the floor, "that one is complicated."

"Do you even know her?"

"Of course I know her. That's farmer Moises's daughter, Moiselle Moises. The first complication is that her father hates *blans*—specifically, Americans. Second complication is that if he's drunk, you can hear him shooting birds, trees, whatever he sees on his farm."

"Is their farm around here?" Trying to appear nonchalant, Robert put his hands in his pocket.

"Yeah, down that way, but don't you get any ideas. Brother, the offer is open for me to take you to the sweet ladies, uncomplicated."

"I promised my father I wasn't going to get involved in anything like that," Robert said, but he didn't mention how he wanted to hold Moiselle's lower lip between his teeth and taste it.

As he walked away from Jean Pierre, he was already thinking of an excuse to give Moiselle should he find their farm. What would he tell her? How would he start the conversation? Half way down the road, he decided he was going to pretend to be looking for his lost dog. *I'm in big trouble.*

After their meeting at the well, Robert walked away from Moiselle elated but not yet ready to name this emotion pulsating through his body. He wished he had had more time to talk with her. Halfway up the dirt road, Robert tipped his hat to a woman on a mule. She had the same flawless dark skin as Moiselle. Her hair was covered by a multicolored scarf. Her chin was more angular. When she saluted Robert, her voice seemed husky, as if it emanated from the back of her throat. He stopped walking and recognized in her face a story his father had told him. It was the two children on the second mule who giggled at his gawking at their mother that gave Robert a way to diffuse his rudeness. The boy, who looked to be about seven, placed his slingshot under his thigh and reached for the rope Robert carried around his shoulder. Robert fake-dodged him.

He followed the wafting smoke back to the church grounds. There was a small white building with two red crosses painted on the side. The green entry doors anchored it back to the brown earth. Although it wasn't a big building, it towered over the hay-thatched cottages surrounding it. He didn't need the light blazing from the open fire pits to see where he was heading. Something to enjoy later, he thought, especially if they stayed outside praying late into the night. He noted the pink line of the darkening horizon and knew his father was going to have comments about his disappearance.

The dinner table was already set up in the yard outside the tent that would be used for tomorrow's revival opening. He intersected with his father, who was heading for the dinner table. Robert maneuvered him away from the gathering dinner attendees. He took off his hat, slapped his father's shoulders. He had not been this happy about news in a long time. "Dad, I think I found her. I saw her."

His father gave a faint smile. He leaned against the wall and gestured for a young maid. She was carrying a bowl of boiled chestnuts toward the dinner table. He reached in a grabbed a handful. "Is this all, Mr. Colvin?" the young girl asked. He answered her with the shaking of his head.

Robert took the cue of the girl's retreating back to continue, "Dad, I'm telling you. The cross on her face was just like you told me." Colvin stopped peeling and popping chestnuts into his mouth. "There are so many of them who put a cross on their faces. I won't ever find her."

"You told me that her cross would be different. That you saved soul her by carving a cross from her right eyebrow, down the bridge of her nose. And I saw her. She said hello to me as she sat on her mule."

"Hush now boy, this is not civil conversation for supper time. Besides, others will be joining us soon."

That was not the response Robert was expecting. Suddenly, Robert backed away and headed in the direction of the pitcher and pail on a table that served as the hand-washing station. When he was done, the hosting pastor, Reverend Denis, a short, jovial man Robert liked to listen to, motioned for him to come sit across from his family. Two deacons were already standing by the table and extended a hand to him. He moved towards his father, and before he had an opportunity to give his excuses for being late, his father cut him off.

"Boy, don't you know you're not a kid anymore? You are a twenty-year-old man! You can't leave work half way done and go exploring. Jean-Pierre an 'em had to finish setting up," his father squealed like a woman.

"Colvin, darling, let him tell his side," Robert's step-mother, Beverly, interjected, but suggestion was brushed off. Robert noted that that was probably the only thing she was going to say all night.

He was happy to have given her that rare opportunity to talk. Robert looked at his father, Pastor Colvin Donner. Once he seemed like a giant, but now Robert looked down to meet his blue gaze. His firm hands moved spasmodically, so often that he held on to edges and shoulders. He shaved his head and when the sun hit his bald head, very often it looked like a pink tomato. His eyes didn't crinkle in mystery and mischievousness like Robert's. They were eyes that looked only into the future, looked at church benches, pulpits, building doors—places for his name.

"I'm sorry. I got lost," Robert muttered, averting his stepmother's flushed face and the hosting pastor's forgiving eyes. A feeling similar to looking at an accident of mangled strangers' bodies came over Robert every time he thought about the petite, round-faced woman his father married five years before.

Robert inhaled the savory smell of stewed meat, and his eyes stopped on the large bowl of rice with red beans—one of his favorites. He didn't pay attention to the white rice and navy bean sauce, and all the other steaming dishes with colorful and aromatic creations. He was relieved when one of the hired young women brought a pitcher of sweet papaya juice. She was about Moiselle's age—fifteen, dark, with a pretty, round face. Why didn't this girl move him like Moiselle did? No other girl had lingered on his mind like this. *Was she a test?* Was she a demon trying to enter his heart and lead him astray from his ministerial calling? His heart dropped. Was this what Jean-Pierre had been trying to tell him about Moiselle being complicated?

There were ten things he mustn't ever do, scribbled on the back page of his Bible. At the top: never engage sexually or marry the locals. He had stared at that list every morning for the past seven years. The second was to never attract the attention of any local police or military official—don't take political sides. Before he could think about the third, the calming voice of Mrs. Denis, the hosting pastor's wife, interrupted his reveries. "Everyone is here now, so my darling, will you say Grace?" Then, she stood behind a chair next to her husband, opposite his father.

Pastor Denis capitalized on his wife's maneuvering of the tension and spoke in short, raspy laughs. "Very well, darling, before we sit to eat, first let me come to the rescue of this dear young man. Not to undermine your authority, Pastor Donner, but let's pray and eat. Disagreements are always less injurious on a full stomach." The clergy and the other four people who had been helping, including Jean-Pierre, took a sit around the long, hand-hewn table.

Robert sat and immediately his father started praying. "Glorious Heavenly Father, bless the hands that cooked this wonderfully smelling meal we're about to eat. Father God, Israel having forsaken your son and not heard his message, you have made us your new chosen people. As such, you have commissioned us to make disciples of our brothers with less opportunities. Give us strength tonight, tomorrow, and in the coming weeks as we try to win souls for you. The devil is an accuser and a liar. He is going to try to confuse us; he will tempt us from the work of our salvation. But Holy Father, we ask you to bind those evil thoughts and tendencies. Jesus bind our thoughts. As always, I pray for the soul of my dearly departed first missus. Keep her soul dear God..."

"Amen, amen," Mrs. Denis said in whispers. It was her third attempt to end Pastor Donner's prayer, but each time his voice grew into a crescendo and then plummeted to the bottom of his vocal range to scrape up more words, roll them into balls, and launch them off the pinnacle of his lamentation.

Inside, Robert cringed each time Mrs. Denis said "Amen". His father's mealtime prayers always took exactly ten minutes—Colvin maintained that anything less felt like cheating God. Robert corralled his thoughts elsewhere. What was Moiselle was doing right now? What was she having for dinner? Was her mother's day at the market successful? Then he chastised himself for having such thoughts during prayer. The question about whether she was a test or a demon returned. When his father stopped, the resounding, "Amen" echoed in the night.

Robert didn't realize he had begun to nibble at a piece of meat until Pastor Denis addressed him. "Robert, you must be in deep thoughts about the Lord. I'm looking forward to your sermon tomorrow. Are you ready?" Pastor Denis's question was filled with too much exuberance for Robert. It didn't bother him that the man was always happy; it bothered him that he thought everyone else should be also. Robert nodded and smiled.

"Of course he's ready. Been trainin' him since he was yea high--13. That was the age Jesus started his ministry, as you know. Every young person ought to commit to serving the Lord wholeheartedly by that age."

"Pastor Donner, you said some lovely things about your first wife in your prayer. How long were you two by yourselves before the Lord blessed you with a new wife?" Denis asked, Robert's fork stopped moving. If this question led to talks about his mother, it was going to unravel his father.

Colvin licked the residue of papaya juice from his upper lip. "I was alone a long time before I met my coy Beverly, here. Before I met my first wife, I was a young US Marine. I remember when we landed here. 1915. People were cheering. We were the answer to many prayers. Sure was. It didn't take long for my back wood Tennessee training to work in my favor. In fact, when I tell people Brentwood, they often think I mean Backwoods." He slapped his thighs in laughter. "My father lived with the Indians dealing furs and pelts. Right he did. He learned things that he taught me that I've learned my boy here," he said, pointing proudly at Robert.

The two deacons, in suits they wore only on Sundays and occasions like this, nodded and hung on Colvin's every word. Maybe they were trying to keep up with his father's accent, the way he mangled words as if wrapping them in a ball of yarn. Denis's teenage sons seemed to have some secret game going on. Robert tried to figure out what the kicks under the table and the different clearings of their throats signified. Two kicks--the white pastor is crazy. Three kicks--let's put a frog in Robert's bed tonight.

"Here's one of those things my father taught me. Look up there. You see that crescent moon? If it has a star near it—on either side—betcha bottom dollar you can expect rain. But we're good tonight. Ain't no star near that moon." The deacons and the pastor's family laughed; Robert and his step-mother kept cutting the fried pork on their plates into smaller pieces.

"I'm not bragging, but it was my commanding officer himself, Chip Williamson Rheich, God bless his soul, who said," Colvin imitated the officer's deep, muddled voice, "He said, 'Donner, you 'bout the best Caco hunter I ever seen.'" He looked at Mrs. Denis who perked up at *Caco hunter*.

"You know 'bout those boys, don't you?" Colvin moved his eyes to Pastor Denis, who gave Pastor Donner an I-know-but-I'm-going-to-act-like-I-don't look. "Dem was the rebels. They started trouble and wasn't letting progress happen. Damn Cacos!"

"Some people think they were heroes against the American's invasion. They were going to enslave us, sir," Mrs. Denis said, half-surprising herself and placing her hand over her mouth.

"Enslave you say? We got our own blacks that we freed, why would we want to enslave your country? We was nice enough to come and help Haiti. Man, this place was a mess before we came. Talk about fighting, corruption, and all kinds of diseases. I was hunting these rebels in the deep woods. I bet I know places here that you don't even know and this is your very own country."

All the Haitians nodded in acquiescence, but exchanged glances that Robert took to mean they were uncomfortable with his father's comments.

Colvin scooped a spoonful of white rice and navy bean sauce. On the way down, the empty spoon shook and clanged against the aluminum tumbler filled with papaya juice. "One day, they sent me after this one local guy. He was armed and dangerous. I laid out my camp. I lived in a hole for six months, waiting for him. Before that

I had spent three months tracking him. I mean he never left any signs when he was somewhere, but he came out at night to hunt. One foggy night, he got snared in my rope. At the break of dawn, I crawled out of my hole and found him howling at his busted ankle. Did I kill him? I did no such thing. I took him back to Port-au-Prince. He was an articulate man. Well-educated and connected. He pleaded with me as we rode back to the capital, but I said no. I stood and watched as they slipped my rope around his neck. You know what his last words were, 'Après moi, le deluge.' *After me comes the flood.* All the way to Port au Prince he kept ranting about our destinies being tied and knotted. I didn't know then what I know now."

The day after Robert and Moiselle met at the well, it was New Year's Day. Moiselle got up early with her mother and peeled pumpkins for soup. She killed two chickens without her mother even having to ask her, and she didn't mention Robert's invitation to the revival again.

She swept the chicken feathers off the dirt kitchen floor as she thought about how she was going to convince her mother to allow her to go to the revival's opening. People went house hopping to taste the customary New Year's Day soup, a celebration tied to Haiti when it became the first Independent Negro nation in the New World. But the only independence Moiselle was thinking of was her own. She saw herself living in her own house with a maid, just like the rich women in Port-au-Prince. She always wished her mother would take her on another trip like that, but there just was never a good time.

The previous New Year's Day, she had had her monthly and her mom let her stay home, where she danced naked in the moonlight. She did not sing church songs. She called on all the *lwas* because unlike the church saints, they know how to make humans have fun. They know how to dance. But this year, she wanted to dance in the moonlight with Robert. When she had finished the last of the dishes, her mother came out to where she sat staring at the road.

"You've done an excellent job helping me today. I'll see if Papa will let you go to that revival, but you have to take Assez-fille and Champagne with you. Be careful with Champagne's ears when you give him a bath. He's been complaining that his ears hurt." Moiselle knew what her mother meant to say was, "Be careful with your father's son whom he named after his beloved hero."

Later, her two siblings in tow, Moiselle half-walked half-ran up the winding path toward the revival tent. She wore her tightest white blouse that gave a peek inside if she moved her shoulders backwards. This she planned to do once she and Robert were alone. A pastor. He will be different. He will be the one to take me out of this boring hell-hole. America. Visions of snow melting into milk, and honey and gold dripping from branches of trees. The gold that made white people's hair so golden. She admonished herself for sounding like an opportunist, but then she reasoned that she did like him and why couldn't she fall in love with someone who could help her dreams come true, she asked herself?

When she reached the revival tent, she sat close to the exit. The kerosene lamps and fire pits were surrounded by worshippers shouting and dancing to the Christian-christened Nago drumbeats, which made the church music sinuous and aggressive. Moiselle let this combination of beats and shouts ensnare her and lift her undulating body off the ground. She closed her eyes in rapture as she moved without inhibition. Her siblings watched in awe and joined in.

In Kreyol, Robert led the part of the service they called "praise-and-worship". Another white man with a very shiny head preached. Moiselle loved the praise and worship. Something about the song, "Roll Calls in Heaven" made her shudder. The sweet recursive melody that gained momentum while allowing space for the drum to vibrate brought her close to tears. Robert looked at her as he played the accordion and she felt like she was being lifted off the ground. She pinched herself not to give into that light, freeing feeling. Some of the neighborhood boys who had converted before she arrived played the drum. She had heard of these brief conversions. Those boys were looking for opportunities like she was, except she was lucky to be a woman--she had more to offer—she reasoned. She was surprised to see among the converts one particular self-proclaimed troubadour whom she knew was a voodoo priest in training. She didn't like the way men like him stared at women, as if they took all of her in one look and didn't give any back. With the same quickness that she backed away from his advances, she averted her eyes from Jean Pierre, who winked at her as if to say, "How do you like me now? One day, you'll be mine."

Moiselle was thankful when Robert came to the pulpit and began to read. "A woman who had a flow of blood for twelve years came from behind and touched the hem of his garment. For she said to herself, 'If only I may touch the hem of His garment, I shall be made well." Then, Robert threw the Bible to the floor. The crowd gasped.

"This is meaningless if you don't believe it! That woman had so much faith that she was healed!" he shouted. He slapped his chest. "My life is not worth living if I don't have Jesus. JESUS!" He jumped into the crowd and the young people jumped up to catch him. They carried him over their heads back to the pulpit, chanting, "Jesus, He is worthy."

The more the crowd moved, the less Moiselle smelled the ginger and cinnamon tea coming from a neighboring yard. Robert seemed to dance and fly and when he appeared in front of Moiselle, she didn't recognize him. His sweat-drenched face, his blond curls plastered to his forehead gave him the look of an aged man. He touched her hand, and she felt deep down in her soul a heat, a fire. She yelled, "Jesus, help me!" and she meant it. She cried, and felt the need for whatever or Whomever moved this crowd to take her along, to lift her up too.

After Robert's sermon, a modest choir sang somber songs that brought a calm over the crowd. Moiselle sat and tried to understand the feelings pulsating through her body. She felt as if she had danced two raras. After the last prayer, and biscuit and teas had been served, she caught Robert's signal to follow him. Moiselle spotted a cousin and told him, "Chango and Assez-fille want to stay and have whatever gifts the white people are giving. I have an upset stomach and am going home, can you take them home later?" He agreed and she walked away thinking and wondering if she had covered all her bases.

Robert had changed his clothes. His curls were dried and his face clean. They walked to the part of the field that was flat. At first they sat looking at the sky, as if words were written up there. She was amazed at how tongue-tied she felt. She didn't want to tell him that seeing him on the stage with that accordion made her want to jump into his arms and have him fold her in and out of his arms like he did to that accordion. She wanted his fingers to glide over her spine the way they tickled those keys. She wondered if his sweat tasted salty like hers. She hoped that he translated her silence as a sign of politeness and was relieved when he began to speak. "I could sing all day, don't you love music?"

She nodded her head and smiled and their fingers brushed. She didn't move away when he closed his enormous hands around hers. The warmth emanating from them melted her reservation. She was at once thankful that he was interested, yet she was scared of spoiling her chance. *What if he thinks I'm dull and stupid? What can I say to this man who knows the Bible, and America, and probably most of Haiti?* She focused on finding a good question. He beat her to it.

"So, what does a pretty girl do with herself all day? I mean, do you go to school, do you have friends, tell me about the mysterious Moiselle."

She giggled and put her palm to her lips. "I used to go to the free missionary school, but my father said they weren't teaching me anything but bad American ideas, so I couldn't go any more. Besides, people don't think teaching girls is a good thing. My very dearest friend, Carline, was sent to Port-au-Prince to go to a real school. I heard that a girl actually graduated from the big university, but my mother complains about why they won't make a law to let girls go to school. So mostly I stay home now." There was more silence until she said, "I enjoyed the music tonight."

"So at least we have one thing in common," he said, intending to be funny.

"Right," she said. "Did you learn to play the accordion here or back in America?"

"Taught myself actually," he said leaning back with his hands as a pillow against the grass littered with frangipani petals.

She was impressed. "I could never teach myself something that complicated."

"Oh, it is simple. I fiddled around with the keys until I learned which keys made what sounds. Let me show you something. Give me your fingers." Moiselle obliged. "Press back each finger that I press and mimic my sound." He pressed on each finger with the tip of his finger.

She enjoyed the soft pressure. Sitting face to face with him as the moon shone behind his head, she confirmed that his hair was as soft and curly as she imagined. She inhaled the frangipani petals. Admiring him caused her to miss a beat on the finger-play.

He laughed and said, "Maybe tomorrow I can show you on the real accordion."

"Was that your father who preached?" she asked, not wanting the conversation to slow.

He stiffened. "What gave it away?" He tossed a piece of grass stalk he had been playing with behind her.

Based on the silence that followed, Moiselle quickly changed the subject. "Are there really rivers of milk in America?"

"I left when I was pretty young, but I never saw any rivers of milk. The only river I knew took my mother's life."

She wanted to reach out and touch his face, but stopped herself for fear of appearing too forward.

He gave a little laugh. "My dad doesn't think the river did it, though."

She gave him a quizzical look.

"He thinks a rope killed her. He thinks it's taken everyone he loved. That rope is one of the reasons why we came to Haiti."

"I don't understand," she said.

"After my mother died--they found her in the river with a rope around her--my father sort of went crazy. He claimed it was the rope he had used to catch a famous Haitian rebel and they used the rope to partly hang the man."

Moiselle put her hand over her mouth. "What was this rebel man's name?"

"Champagne or something like that?" Moiselle looked as if Robert had dropped a ten pound stone on her head. When the warmth returned in her veins, she said, "Chango Champagne is my father's hero. My father was one of Champagne's recruits. He loved him so much he named my brother after him." They paused and looked at each other in silence, and then Robert mumbled quietly, as if in pain, "Complicated, complications."

"Seven-year-old Robert was up a tree as muddy waters raged below. The water was coming. We had known for a few hours. Neighbors had warned at dawn that several neighboring towns were flooded," Colvin said to Pastor Daniel Denis, who had come to pray with him.

"Pastor Colvin, I don't know if you should be telling stories. You preached a great sermon yesterday at the New Year's night service, but you've been running a fever all day today. You should save your energy, sir."

"Fever? I'm as cold as Satan's tit. Boy, pull up a chair and hear about these stories. Write them down. I won't be around forever."

"Come on, Pa, your soup is getting cold," Robert said as he leaned over his father, a bowl of soup in one hand and a spoon in the other. "You don't want your sugar to drop in the middle of the night. Why don't you save the rest of the story for tomorrow?" Robert twirled the pieces of vegetables in the pumpkin soup. Pastor Denis sat uncomfortably at the foot of the bed.

Colvin tapped on the side table with the tips of his fingers. What did Colvin know or did he suspect? Robert wondered. *That a rebel put a voodoo curse on him and his life has been tied up ever since he captured the man?* Robert could recite the story. As Colvin moved from one tangent to another, Robert felt more embarrassed. *Whatever happened to rule number six: reveal as little as possible about yourself to the natives?* His gaze remained on the flame in the fireplace where burning logs expanded and made popping sounds.

"Well, they had used my rope to string Champagne up. After that, they tied him to a door and put him on display for the whole world to see. Soon I discovered they had taken his picture and mass produced it. Every street and every wall in Port-au-Prince had a picture of the dead Champagne tied up to that door with my rope."

By this point in Colvin's recursive story-telling, one of the maids had returned. The incredulous look on her face upon hearing part of the story was like half of an equation whose other half was on Pastor Denis' face. However, Colvin was on to a scent, a hunt, a kill.

Colvin continued, "I stayed for four more years and finally got my real ropes. When my tour of duty was over, I made my way home from New York and the bus broke down in Louisville. So, picture this: I'm waiting for the replacement bus heading to Tennessee when a young girl, about seventeen, comes walking into the almost empty bus station. As God planned, she was waiting for the same bus too. I mean she was a beauty. Milky white skin without a spot on it and the reddest lips I ever seen on any woman not wearing lipstick. I can see her now in that light green dress and white hat and shoes. She looked sharp." Colvin stopped and looked off in a distance. Holding his shaking hands up a bit, pointing at a scene only visible to him, he said, "Right there I fell for Violet Johnson. We talked non-stop on that ten-hour bus ride. When we got off the bus, I got on my knees and I proposed. She accepted my proposal and we walked to her grandparents' house. And on account of me being in my uniform, I impressed them so much they gave me their blessings right there. I stayed with them and in less than a week we were married."

Pastor Denis smiled at Colvin, waiting for more, and then finally clapped his hands together and said in a cheerful voice, "What God puts together, let no man put asunder". He and Robert clapped for the joy that the story might be at an end. Colvin said, "Praise the Lord. You can say that again. But you know those first years were tough. Try as I did, I wasn't able to find work in Chattanooga—that's where Violet's grandparents lived and that's where we stayed after we got married. I bought my first car, a 1909 Ford T model. It was red with white wheels no thicker than what we put on bicycles now. The top folded back like an accordion. It had an orange-sized peekaboo hole on the back that you looked out of when the top was up. It was over fifteen years old, but it purred like a cat when cranked right. It belonged to Violet's grand-daddy, but I didn't take it as a weddin' present. Later when I found work, I paid him over $200 for it."

Pastor Denis got up again to leave, but Colvin reached for his sleeve and said, "My friend, you don't wanna miss what I'm about to say." Denis sat back down.

"Well, people started moving away north. The dust rose from the ground and beat us down. I had never seen something like that. We packed up everything we had and headed towards Ohio because it was supposed to be better there. It took a week and we ran out of money. We started eating, believe it or not, boiled grass and grasshoppers. Violet was worried sick and scared for the life growing inside her. On that road, my beautiful boy here was born. Then Violet took ill. I stopped at a little town right off the Ohio River. We stayed in a little shack fit only for keeping animals, but it was free. All I had to do was help the widowed owner one day a week. All the time we were going through our misery, I kept thinking about Haiti. There is something about this place that knows how to take misery out of anything and make it better. Seems like life was better for me in Haiti—I kept thinkin' and sayin' to myself. Even when I was in the hole tracking that rebel, I could count on my stash or rations. Everythin' was pointin' me towards returnin' to Haiti. Well, I told Violet that I wanted to return to Haiti and I had a feeling they were better off than we were in America. People kept sayin' we were in a depression—American Depression—like it was some soup to put on a menu. After the baby was born we kept heading north. I took in work at any farm that would take us three—even if we had to sleep in that car. Sometimes I had to push that car for miles it seems.

"When Robert was about five, looked like things were starting to pick up. I had found steady work on a farm in Lionsville, right off the Ohio River, closer to the West Virginia side. This gave us steady food. In two years, even though we had very little, Violet managed to make our little shot gun home into a paradise. She took in people's washes and yet the house always smelled like cinnamon apple pies. She kept a garden of flowers in the front and vegetables in the small yard.

"One July day, a steady rain kept me out of the fields. I welcomed the chance to stay home since I rarely did. Violet was making pies and Robert was singing a hymn from church while banging on some cans. We heard a horrible sound. Like the world's shell breaking and we are the yolk. The water sounded angry as it barreled through the farm, snagglin' every structure. Ever heard metal crying? Nails, screws, studs popping out of trusses. Small trees forced to their knees as each rain drop banded together to occupy the land. The animals knew best; they just didn't fight—let the water take them where ever.

"The Ohio River flooded us and everyone out in Lionsville. Right away the sweet smells of cinnamon and apples and flowery front yard was replaced by the meanest stench you ever wanna know. You know, even now as I tell you this, I can see our little shot gun shack sinking. Our old car submerged. When the water came through the door and window, I ran for Robert. My thinking was to get Robert and come back for my wife, but the water had already reached her in the kitchen. I swam to a tree and put Robert there and told him to climb to the highest branch. I dived back in and couldn't see her. The water was already murky. The stench of busted out houses and the things from out-houses just floating around. My heart sank when I didn't see the house. The water had taken it away.

"A day later, when the water receded, we found her. A rope just like the rope that had been around that rebel's neck was around her. At once I recognized that this was the work of the devil and I said, 'I rebuke thee in the name of Jesus!' That was the night I gave my life to Jesus.

"How can this be that this man sent a flood to pluck my Violet from my arms? This is why I pray for her soul. Every day, five times a day." Colvin was in tears, shaking. A prayer broke from

Pastor Denis and his wife who had joined them in the middle of the story. Robert never raised his head, his eyes flooded with water too, suddenly the rope at his feet tightened.

*****

Seven-year-old Robert straddled a branch near the top of a sprawling eucalyptus tree. He wondered why the branches were still bare on this early summer morning. He knew that trees grew leaves in the summer and they fell in the fall. He looked at the tree and marveled at how he never noticed it before until that very moment that he needed it. "Stop dreamin' boy at a time like this and move your butt to the top of that tree," his father shouted. Robert moved to a higher branch. Then Colvin climbed on top of a piece of floating metal that had been part of some roof. On his knees, Colvin paddled frantically and used bigger objects floating within his reach to gain leverage. The goats and sheep were the loudest. Robert wondered if their bleating was complaints, promises, or reprimands to Mother Nature like he was doing in his mind. The cows floated by as if swimming. They didn't fight the water.

A dog paddled by holding onto a human leg. Robert turned his head, not wanting to see if the leg was attached to a living or dead person. After his father became smaller and smaller, an entire roof floated by with two young men on top. "Hey boy, jump down and swim here. Come with us."

"My Pa be right back. He'd be real mad if he didn't find me here," he shouted and made no move to climb down. Then panic grabbed him. What if Pa doesn't come back? What if he forgets what tree I'm in? "Pa! Pa!" he screamed, scaring off the birds in two neighboring smaller trees. He called for his father until he felt as if boiled hot water was being poured down his throat. Then a putrid smell rose from the river and punched him in the throat. He coughed into the peeling bark of the tree and tried to smell the bark, but the new scent of the flood had cloaked him. Thumps and moans seemed to come from the bottom of the river. Were those the sounds of people trapped in houses or sunken boats? He shook his head, refusing to imagine scary things.

The sun was lower in the sky. It looked like a yellow piece of bread someone was dunking in the murky flooded plain. Robert wondered if his father found his mother. He closed his eyes, not wanting to cry. He pictured his mother's soft hands when she tucked his hair behind his ears. He saw her in the garden whistling. He promised himself that he wouldn't ever complain again when she asked him to help her boil the jars for canning or go to a neighbor's house with a container of jam or some cucumbers to barter for something they didn't have.

Robert tried to imagine the taste of his mother's pumpkin pie. He decided that the first thing he would ask her to make would be a pumpkin pie. Just then something floated slowly past the tree. Robert recognized the apron. She wore the purple gingham apron every day. Reluctantly, his eyes traveled up the length of her body. She was tangled in ropes. She was on her back, her arms sprawled open, the rope around her torso and neck. He scrambled down the branch, shouting, "Ma! Ma! Hold on...grab my hands Ma!" But she had already floated past the tree, not struggling. Her eyes were a beacon fixed at the sky. He climbed back up to the top branch, screaming "Mama!" He didn't care that he sounded like a baby. He didn't care that only screeches come out of him. Later, when sounds refused to come out of his throat, he saw the leaf. There was a leaf. The tiny fuzz of the leaf gave it the look of a silver dollar. He crumpled it, marveling at its crunchiness despite the wetness and sogginess of everything around him. The smell opened the image of his mother's garden, and she was that great big tree cradling him above the murky waters.

A mild ray of sun, still pink with possibilities, streamed through the small, glassless window of the room Robert shared with Pastor Denis's three children. *Thank God this is temporary.* He looked at the star apple on the window sill, and marveled at how after ten days, the fruit was intact. Ten days had passed, and he knew it was a matter of time before his heart accepted what his mind knew had to be done.

Robert flipped onto his back and something poked him through the cotton mattress. He felt lucky to have a bed to himself. He didn't have to look at the three boys in the bed across from him--he knew that two of them would be hanging vertically on the edge of the bed, and the youngest would be balled up in the middle.

Robert made a mental note of all the things he had to do and began to rouse. Judging by the light outside he knew he had less than thirty minutes to hitch a ride with the only car for at least twenty miles. The night before, as he had supported his father from the dinner table to his bed, his father had told him to retrieve the mail and a parcel from Port-au-Prince. He said, "Robert, don't you dare talk religion to that priest. Be respectful, but you know the Catholics. Closet voodoo practitioners that's what they are. Add that to your notes, son," he implored, holding Robert's hands firmly.

"I will Dad, I will," Robert said, a refrain he knew all too well.

While his father's words hung in his mind, a figure riding a donkey appeared in the distance and he thought of Moiselle. That night, sitting in that field, he found out just how complicated it would be with her. However, he couldn't stop thinking about her. The way she threw her head back in laughter. The way she covered her mouth with one hand when she was embarrassed. Even though he promised himself not to pursue her, he was excited about the possibility of seeing her later that day at the open-air church ceremony. He had finished putting on his shoes when he heard conversation outside. Moiselle was holding the reins of her donkey and talking to Mrs. Denis.

Ten days after the New Year's Day Revival, Moiselle arrived at the church compound and laid out her mat in front of the white-washed stone wall. She thought often of the way Robert had left the field abruptly, mumbling an apology and talking about some lily and complications as he ran back towards the revival tent. *Didn't the white shirt show enough? Maybe I should have asked fewer questions.* At the front of the church, she chose a spot where she could be seen by anyone in the compound, but far enough from the dirt road that she wouldn't be caught in any dust storm created by cars or animals.

"To what do I owe this occasion?" Mrs. Denis asked Moiselle, who was busy piling her fruits and vegetables into pyramids.

"Good morning, Mrs. Pastor," Moiselle said, wringing her hands. Mrs. Denis stood with her arms crossed and smiling, revealing a slim gold grill around one of her front two teeth. "My donkey doesn't look like he's going to make it to the market. So, if it's all right with you, can I set up my merchandise here today?"

"Moiselle, as I live and breathe. You think I was born yester-day. Girl, your mother wouldn't approve of what you're doing here. Don't you know a girl shouldn't chase a man?"

"Mrs. Pastor, I don't know what you're talking about--"

"...She says so innocently with those big beautiful eyes like her mother. Child, did your mother ever tell you that we were initiates together?" Moiselle shook her head. Mrs. Denis picked up an orange from the first pile and gave her a red coin. They stood side by side as several women making their way to market on donkeys yelled the standard salutation, "Honor" at both of them. They waived back, saying "Respect". Amidst the clatter of hooves breaking stones, children crying, braying donkeys, and sing-song salutations, the two shared the orange.

Then they sat with green, red, and orange pyramids of fruits between them. Moiselle noted how flexible the older woman was as she folded her legs under her long skirt. "Your mother and I had some good times when we were about your age. The mambo whom we studied under was Piti. She never told you? Your poor mother. She is probably so tired from planting her garden, cooking, cleaning, washing, and raising you three to even talk. Thank God I married the right man. I have someone to help with the wash, the cooking, and the children. Little girl, you've got to marry the right person. You hear."

Moiselle shook her head in acquiescence. She wondered if Mrs. Denis had her hair in that bun as a child. "My mom did tell me she learned to worship the spirit with Piti."

"Child, is that what she calls it? It's voodoo. We used to worship that stupidity, but now I found God and He put the right man in my path, but yes, Piti was our manbo mother. Big woman with a name that means small. She was wonderful," Mrs. Denis shooed a fly and Moiselle noted that for the fifth time she used her index finger to remove something that wasn't at the corner of her eyes. The only thing that interrupted the smoothness of her brown face were the darker circles under her eyes. Un-phased by Moiselle's stare, she continued, "Even if you hate dogs, you must admit they have white teeth. Those voodoo societies are good to orphans. There were many of us whose fathers had been forced by the Americans to go into labor camps. Our fathers died or never returned. Some of us when we turned fourteen and fifteen after five or six years into the occupation, we joined the fight." Moiselle tried to look as if this was old information, but her mother never talked about her parents. In fact, she thought, neither of her parents discussed their lives before they met and got married here in Croix des Bouquets.

"I'll tell you a funny story," Mrs. Denis said as a mild burp escaped her slim, brown lips. "Sorry. Oh where was I. The funny story, right. See, one day your mother had to do a special dance for a visiting ougan and she forgot her head wrap. The only clean thing around was one of Piti's big underwear and a spare dress—I guess for Piti to change into after the dance ceremony. The dress was too big for what she needed. Your mother used the underwear and styled it so nicely. Child, no one guessed! When Piti realized it, she laughed and dubbed your mother Panty- head. From that time on, your mother could not shake that name."

Moiselle chuckled trying to imagine her mother, who rarely smiled now, laughing. Her smiled turned serious when she saw Pastor Denis standing in the distance. The pail in his hand had red paint that seemed to be leaking from the side. In the distance, he waved the red brush in the air and his wife waved back. Moiselle noted that her smile wasn't as wide as it had been before. "Pastor is painting?" Moiselle asked not seeing anything red on the church's ground. Mrs. Denis turned her gaze to an approaching boy and said, "Something like that. Something like that."

"I've come to buy tomatoes and carrots," a young boy of about eight interrupted.

"This is how you come up on people who are older than you?" Mrs. Denis reprimanded.

"I'm sorry, Auntie," the boy said and corrected himself, "Honor."

"Respect," Mrs. Denis and Moiselle responded in unison. The boy handed Moiselle two small silver coins and she handed him five carrots and four tomatoes. The boy carried the items in the crook of his arm as if they were a baby. Moiselle and Mrs. Denis watched the boy's retreating back as a vulture circled.

"Something near is dead," Moiselle quipped pointing to the bad news bird circling.

"Maybe, but since we cleared out the trees for the revival, they've had no place to rest and congregate. Speaking of the revival, I watched you at the last one. Robert seemed to play that accordion in front of you most of the night. So seeing you here now, I figured it out."

"But there is nothing to figure out, Auntie."

"I hope you took something Godly from the revival. You young people are always looking for love like it's hidden under some rock." She threw her head back and small laughs escaped her drying lips. "Have you ever noticed that an image in the mirror equals what is standing in front of the mirror?" Moiselle nodded. "Love is the mirror and when it is real love, it won't matter whether you or the one you choose is the image or the reflection. If you seek God, He will give you the right husband. But if you seek the husband without God, all you might get is a man who gives you the right hand across the face."

Moiselle lowered her eyes, thinking of the way her father's right hand sometimes found her mother's face.

"You know how people talk, Moiselle. Your mother probably already knows you didn't reach the market and you stationed out here now. If you play your cards right and take God seriously, it might end differently than the Chin boy and that silly ring you wore around your neck."

Moiselle eyes opened wide as they met Mrs. Denis' daring gaze. Moiselle nervously reached for the orange peel and squeezed the zest out of it.

"How is old Mr. Chin anyway?"

"China," she blurted, knowing it wasn't the right answer to the question. "He took his son back to China."

"Probably to marry a Chinese girl after that boy done drink the nectar of some of our best flowers. The nerve. Well, Mr. Chin is not half as bad as those other foreigners. At least he gives back."

"Honor," came a breathless voice. The tall, skinny woman placed the basket she'd been carrying on her head down as Moiselle and Mrs. Denis responded, "Respect."

"Mrs. Pastor, don't you want to see some of the lovely fabrics I've got from Port-au-Prince. Just arrived and at a good price." The vendor draped argyle, gingham, and floral in hues of orange and red over her ebony arm.

"Ooh, Pratique. How much for this piece?" Mrs. Denis inquired, pointing to the floral.

"The usual," the vendor said, not looking at Moiselle whose eyes were on a yellow and red paisley design.

"I have a piece of that cloth big enough to make a nice skirt for you," the vendor said to Moiselle.

"This is my mother's money, Auntie."

"I need carrots, tomatoes, and some sweet potatoes. We could work something out."

Moiselle piled eight carrots and tomatoes and four boniato in a pile. "My mother won't miss this."

The vendor swooped down and put the items at the bottom of her basket and gave Moiselle the piece of cloth. Then she retreated, singing and waving at every passing woman, "Today, Pratique chou-chou, good prices. Straight from the Port-au-Prince."

As she retreated, Mrs. Denis said, "She gave you enough for a nice dress."

"Yes, maybe I'll do it by hand or maybe I'll wait until Mr. Chin comes back to use his sewing machine." Moiselle stared blankly at a place in the future when the dress was completed.

"Good old Mr. Chin," Mrs. Denis clapped her hands as if to reinforce the fact that this was the topic she wanted to discuss. "I'm sure your parents never told you this, but your father used to be a fighter, but some people call them rebels—Caco."

Moiselle nodded as if to say tell-me-something-I-don't-know.

"Child, the story goes that around the time Champagne was captured, they captured your father too. The Americans brought him here to work on the water project Mr. Chin had been overseeing. After a while he couldn't help but like Mr. Chin. So on the day some of the men were going to blow up the levy, he kept Mr. Chin at home. Mr. Chin didn't rat him out. In fact, Mr. Chin gave him money to buy his land and the adjacent lot. Your father intending to be funny called it the Promised Land. Does this sound familiar to you?"

"I think it's just another one of those stories people who are jealous of our farm made up," Moiselle said, feigning indignation.

"Child, true or not, it shows that people accept Mr. Chin because he really helps. But I don't know about these other foreigners. They only marry their own kind. In fact, I was curious to see if Pastor Colvin and his son were different. I knew them from five years ago and he didn't have a wife then. So, recently at dinner I asked him about his new wife. Child, the man told me everything in the book of Job except for the real answer. He even claimed that Champagne put a curse on him and killed his wife. Every year you see three or four of these pale women come off the boat. Soon, they will send this boy a wife too."

Moiselle looked away, thankful that her eyes were too dry to mist. Mrs. Denis stopped when a green little car drove slowly by them. Robert looked through the back window at Moiselle who stared at him without blinking once, as if she was seeing someone else. In her deja-vu vision, two other faces and their slanting eyes retrieving in that same car—leaving her and her dreams behind.

****

Robert heard the loud purring of Father Moran's car entering the churchyard. He ran to the car trying not to wake any of the Denis boys.

"You're the lad Jean-Pierre said is needing a ride to Port-au-Prince?" Father Moran asked. He sat in the back of the snug, frog-green Citroen. The interior of the car smelled like lemons, and Robert thought of the name of the car being so close to the French word for lemon—citron—and he smiled to himself. *Do they all smell like lemons?* Once he was seated, Father Moran said to the driver, "Jean-Pierre, don't take the long route, please." Robert noted that Jean Pierre looked different in his uniform shirt and hat. How unlike the carefree guitar playing musician and self-proclaimed healer. Father Moran was dressed differently too, in a suit. As if reading Robert's thoughts, the priest said, "I've been invited to say a prayer at a breakfast being given in honor of the president." Robert nodded at Pastor Moran, thankful that Jean Pierre wasn't driving too fast so that he could look at Moiselle through the window. She was sprawled on a straw mat with colorful piles of fruits in front of her. Her gaze unflinching. He wondered if he was reading too much into the look. Was it anger or sadness? No, he thought the look mirrored that of a Venus fly trap; it was a lay-upon-me-butterfly-I-dare-you look.

A few miles down the road, the dawn and dew cast a pinkish, thick web that opened like the parting of cotton for the little Citroen. Ten minutes later, the whir of the engine lulled Robert to sleep. He woke to Jean-Pierre shaking him gently.

"I already dropped Father Moran off. He should be done in a couple of hours. So I will stay here with the car." Two young boys gesturing and whistling at the car passed so close that if Jean-Pierre had not placed his body between them and the car they would have scratched it. "If this car gets scratched, I will never hear the end of it. His son is a big executive and bought it for him." Robert's face must have shown his shock because he added, "Yeah, well some priests like Moran leave the priesthood to get married, have kids, and then they come back when they're old. Some people think it is safer that way for everyone, don't you think?"

His father would agree Robert thought, but decided to change the subject. He joked, "You look like a serious person in this uni-form. I'm glad you've got an excuse for your laziness."

"Ha, ha, ha. I told Pastor Denis I was going take care of you. Besides, he is excited about this shipment of Bibles."

"Right," Robert laughed, hoping to mask his uneasiness. He couldn't tell Jean-Pierre all that was in the shipping crate.

"It's eight o'clock now. Father Moran wants to be back in Croix des Bouquets by 1:30, so don't wander around and get lost. Here's a map of the depot where the crate is being held. Show them this letter with the church's seal, pay this tax, and get a receipt. They usually take about an hour to bring the crate to the front of the shipping depot. Come back here and I'll bring the car around. We'll load the Bibles together."

"Okay," Robert said. If Jean-Pierre knew so much why hadn't he been the one sent to handle everything? Then, he remembered his father's list of the ten things he should never do. Number three was: Don't trust anyone who is not your blood with a secret. The fact that his father revealed the secrets about the Bibles to Robert was a sign that his father finally realized he was becoming a man. It took a lot not to share the secret with Jean-Pierre. Robert followed up with a handshake he was sure Jean-Pierre wouldn't reciprocate if Father Moran were around.

He crossed the already bustling Harry Truman Boulevard. He was not surprised that such a nicely laid out street was named after an American president. Jean-Pierre would claim that it's because the United States is the new colonial power of the Western Hemisphere. Robert would defend the U.S., but all the while wanting to agree with Jean-Pierre.

Most of the cars whizzing by had black drivers and white passengers--American, French, and Canadian. Robert stood for a moment taking it all in. Rows of royal palm trees lined the streets, their bases painted white. They were so tall that he stood for a long time, looking up. A gust came from the ocean and tousled the heads of the gigantic palms. Small pink and red flowers planted at their bases reminded pedestrians to watch their step. He touched the white paint. He expected it to come off, but it didn't. He tried to remember the last time he was in Port-au-Prince. He was with his father. He had been thirteen and it was at the start of his training or "ministering" as his father liked to call it. Those days his nose was mostly in the Bible. He didn't remember seeing any of what he was seeing now.

On the left of the boulevard, a sign read, "Coming in December 1949—Italian Plaza." The artist's rendition showed water flowing from the fountains, shooting toward a prodigious sky. In the fountain were ebony mermaids, playing with babies on their laps. If he had the money or knew the artist, he would pay to put Moiselle's beautiful face on one of those statues. The plaza was to be built within four years. Robert liked the way the boulevard stretched out before him now, but he saw how this development and its fountains and stores would appeal mostly to white shoppers.

He walked toward the wharf in search of the depot. On the way he passed the Theatre Verdure--dancing men in white, baggy, knee-length pants and women with their heads wrapped in colored cloths that stood stiffly in the air. Further down, he nodded a silent greeting at a man who stood in front of the Coq D'or with a nicely preened burgundy colored rooster. Robert looked back twice to see if the bird was real. The man sang and talked to it, a pep talk before the rooster's fight. He wanted to watch, but not today.

He turned onto a cobbled side street as the map indicated, and walked down to the entrance of the depot. The front was situated on Moises Street–Moiselle!—and the back on Rue L'amour. He smiled.

Street vendors were setting up fruit stands across from a blue door. A couple of men stood waiting. Occasionally, one of them made a remark to the other. When Robert stepped closer, one said, "Don't bother rushing, man. This depot is supposed to be opened at eight, but it won't for another hour. I'm used to these jerks—Haitian time." The complaining man's brown forehead shone like a wet calabash. The other man had a quick smile and Robert decided he was probably an easy person to get along with. His mustache covered his entire upper lip; he shifted his hat from hand to hand.

After fifteen more minutes had passed, the man with the mustache volunteered, "I'm gonna find a street vendor, get me some *akasan*, and watch the ships come in or leave." Robert decided that was a good idea. The three men walked to a vendor on the wharf facing the ocean. Robert paid ten cents for a sweet, milky porridge-like drink. The vendor included two warm, buttered Haitian biscuits. Robert sat looking at the ocean and eating, silent as the other two men engaged in local politics.

"I'm glad they're letting them go back to their country; finally, our white president understands he is dealing with a black country," the man with the mustache said, pointing toward a group of people three or four hundred feet away. Then, realizing the weight of his words, he clarified, "Nothing against white people, man."

Robert smiled an uneasy smile. He still didn't understand what they were talking about. He had once seen a picture of President Stenio Vincent and could see how the men could think of Vincent as white. Mustache man continued, "Did you hear why President Stenio is finally showing his balls?" Both Robert and the other man gave a blank look. "Well, did you know that our president comes from the same whorish mother as the Dominican president Trujillo?"

"I knew it! I had always heard that and thought it was a rumor. True sons of a whore these presidents," the akasan vendor interjected, his glee evident by the congratulatory handshake he gave mustache-man. Mustache-man continued, "Whatever Trujillo does, his brother copies. Trujillo imports white people from Europe to whiten his Dominicans, our president imports Syrians. But we Haitians think coffee should stay black." The men laughed.

Robert didn't really like the trajectory of the conversation.

The short man said, "I heard a rumor that some guerillas kidnapped our president's wife and children. They won't release them until every Syrian is kicked out the country."

Mustache-man nodded, "That's not a rumor my friend. That's a reality. Every day they're leaving by the boat load. Look at them. They hate us. You give them an inch, they will take over the whole island. Piranhas!"

Short-stocky man rubbed the bald spot on his head as if this was a way for him to remember something that needed to be added to this concoction, "Don't tell me you haven't heard that since our president is deviating from the program, Trujillo's killing Haitians and sending them back from the Dominican Republic."

Finally, mustache-man looked surprised.

As Robert finished eating, the men said they were going to watch a cock fight. He didn't have enough for the entry fee, so they parted ways. "Maybe I'll see you back at the depot," Robert told the other men as they shook hands. He decided to walk toward the loading boats and maybe get some answers about what the men were discussing earlier.

Less than two hundred yards from where Robert and the men had purchased their morning porridge, a somber line of women, children, and men moved as if on an assembly track. Robert stared at their faces for a long time. Some looked like the Spaniards he and his dad had met when they travelled to the north of Haiti a few years back. He recognized their olive skin. Three tables were set up about fifteen feet apart. The people moved slowly, getting papers stamped. Those who reached the last table received a small bag and they were escorted to board the boat. Most of the people in line were dressed as if going to church except the women wore black hats—not one had a colorful hat. How different, Robert noted, than if it were a line of Haitian women. The men wore black suits and the boy-children were in dress slacks, suspenders, and bow-ties. The little girls looked like the somber mothers in miniature. *What was so bad about those people?*

A little boy whose well-brushed head gleamed in the sun flew his kite nearby, squinting against the sun. His brown hands and yellowed fingertips glided and tugged expertly at the taut line. Robert watched the wind dance with the red and blue kite, as if it were showing the kite how to tame rhythm. The boy walked slowly on the edge of the sidewalk, his eyes fixed on the roving kite. A few times he stepped into the road. Once he bumped into a cigarette vendor's wooden cart and caused the vendor to go into a shrieking match with the boy. After the boy gained his composure, the kite was back soaring in the sky. Robert marveled at the height and control the boy had. If he squinted, the kite seemed to be as tall as the mountains that suddenly appeared when the clouds parted over

Port-au-Prince. The kite filled in white spaces like a paintbrush, coloring the sky a pinkish gray.

Suddenly, Robert heard screeching brakes. He turned to see a careening car. The little boy continued to fly the kite. A man jumped out in front of the fast moving car, screaming, "Out of the way!" The man pushed the child out of the way. The thud of the boy's body echoed in Robert's mind. The car hit the man. He flew about twenty feet in the air and his head landed first on the edge of the sidewalk. Blood ran like tears from his opened eyes. "God be merciful!" a woman with a black lace scarf around her head chanted as she ran towards the mangled body on the floor. By this time the blood gushed out of the side of the man's head. The boy's mouth hung open. A couple of people pushed the boy out of the way so they could have a closer look at the man. He got down on all fours to retrieve his trampled kite. Robert judged from the boy's tears, as he carried his garbled kite, that he didn't understand that he was the lucky one today.

God-be-merciful woman removed a yellow and blue scarf from around her neck and began to wipe the injured man's face. Then she removed her hat and fanned him. When blood trickled out of the man's mouth, she began to scream, "Somebody help us! For the love of God, help us!" A police officer in his khaki top and dark green uniform approached her. She didn't see him. She was whispering a half song, half complaint to the dying man in an unfamiliar language. The police officer lifted her off the dead man's body. "That's my husband," she shouted in a heavy accent.

"Madame, Madame." The officer's brown fingers around the woman's meaty, pale arms reminded Robert of sausages and gravy. "You're not safe on the street. We have stopped traffic and will get the body moved."

"I want my husband!" the woman sobbed.

"He can go with you. We'll make sure to tell the captain to take good care of the body."

A bystander, arms akimbo next to Robert commented, "Those Syrians will do anything to stay here." Robert backed away, words like fallen kites stuck in his throat.

Finally, closer to eleven, the depot opened. The worker didn't speak to Robert, only stretched out his hand. Robert gave him the church's papers and was told to wait outside again. Half an hour later the attendant returned. "A shipment of Bibles, powdered milk, and beans. Please sign here," he pointed. Robert signed and paid the fees and gave the attendant the extra money as his father had told him to do. The attendant looked around and then pocketed the extra cash.

Robert walked through the depot's exit and was surprised to find Jean-Pierre already waiting outside of the blue depot doors. As he and Jean-Pierre unloaded the food products, he looked for the red Bibles, the ones with hollowed cores that contained monies collected from different churches to support the missionaries. This was the safest way to send money his father told him. Thankfully the secret hadn't been discovered. Knowing how curious Jean-Pierre could be, Robert offered him a free, un-hollowed Bible. "No, thanks, man, I already have three." Shrugging, Robert placed the four cash-filled Bibles in his satchel and the rest in the car's trunk.

From the depot, the streets meandered and got narrower as they moved away from the ocean. Along the road, every five minutes or so, they spotted a line of men, women, and children with knapsack on their backs. "What's going on over there?' Robert pointed to the line of people silently trudging.

"They're the lucky ones who escaped from the Dominican Republic. They went over there to cut cane and now the president of the Dominican Republic, Trujillo, is kicking all the black-skinned Haitians out. Word is he is planning to kill the rest who won't leave. They've overstayed their welcome."

Jean-Pierre rambled on and Robert thought back to the two guys he had met at the depot earlier. Could they have been telling the truth?

Robert and Jean-Pierre finally arrived at the sprawling two-story gingerbread house where the president was being honored and Father Moran had been an honored guest. Six armed men met them at the gate with rifles over their shoulders.

"I'm Father Moran's driver picking him up. This is another man of the cloth."

One of the soldiers turned to ask for clarification on who Father Moran was and if someone would go to retrieve him. "Park that car under the tree until he comes back," the soldier barked and in one fluid motion, the formation turned away and marched to stand guard in the front of the house.

As they waited for the priest, Robert opened a note and photograph wrapped in blue satin that was tucked inside of the blue envelope addressed to him or his father. The note read,

Dear Pastor Donner,

The Lord's grace be upon you. We have made sure to ship these resources a month before the arrival of Ms. White.

Truly, Elder John Jones

Robert looked at the picture. Ms. White seemed like a serious young woman wearing a lavishly decorated hat over blonde, cascading curls. She wore a long skirt, and although the picture was black and white, he knew the skirt wasn't in color. She seemed like she was photographed in another era. On the back was written: Missionary, Sister Lily Ann White. *So this is the girl they are sending for me to marry.*

"You got your shipment?" Father Moran asked cordially as he opened the car door, interrupting Robert's thoughts. Robert replaced the note and picture and closed his satchel. "Yes, sir," he responded curtly with a polite smile.

"Jean-Pierre, take me back to my Croix." The old man laid his head against the felt lining of the car's seat. Robert thought of the Syrian man who jumped in front of a car and gave his life for the little Haitian boy. Suddenly it occurred to him that choosing to pursue Moiselle over the arranged marriage with Lily White was

like jumping in front of a moving car. But, oh those plum lips called
to him.

The night Robert returned from retrieving Bibles in Port-au-Prince, he decided if Moiselle came to another church meeting, he would tell her that he had a duty to his father by marrying someone who was just like him—Ms. White. So how had he gotten from the pulpit to the river bank where he was now captive by her laughter?

"I like what you said tonight about God's paint brush; it was beautiful," she whispered. Robert wondered if all the sugar in her voice was a way to cajole him back to the easiness that had existed between them before she told him about her father being a Cacos—before he had left the field a week and half ago, mumbling about complications and white lilies.

He smiled and took a deep breath. What if he gave her one or two good memories, he wondered, would it be bad? Would it be enough for him? As she threw question after question at him, he caught the easiest one, "How come you speak Kreyol so well?"

"Well, remember I told you that my father believes that the rope found around my mother was the same rope he had been given as a memento? Well, after my mom died, my dad was mostly drinking. A man named Benjamin brought food from his wife. He took me to church, prayed with Dad, cleaned the house, and pretty much took care of us for almost two years. I considered him my dad's best friend. The only problem was, he was a black man, and that kind of friendship was unusual—even forbidden.

"One day, Benjamin went into town to buy some groceries. Dad was home—drunk. Some good-for-nothing losers started to harass Benjamin. They called him "boy" and "George".

"Why George?"

"George is another racist term in my country for black men. It's as bad as calling a black man 'boy'. Anyway, they chased him all the way back to our house and then they beat on him. Well, to make a long story short, my father staggered from his stupor, that rope wrapped around his shoulders like a feathered boa. "What's all the ruckus?" he said, twirling the rope around.

"Mind your own business, nigga-lover!" one of the men holding Benjamin spouted. I was looking through the window, praying that they would not grab the rope and hang my dad. He wasn't as drunk as I thought because he swiftly grabbed a bottle that had been lying on the porch and broke it over one of those men's heads. "Now my aim ain't too good right now, so I suggest you back off. Or you will see your maker tonight."

They backed away, promising, "We'll be back nigga lover. You can count on that."

My father dropped the rope to help Benjamin to the rickety rocking chair on the porch. Benjamin was bleeding at the mouth. I came out with the towel and water my father hollered for me to bring. He washed and cleaned his friend's face. Benjamin held the towel down to stop the bleeding. We waited and when the blood stopped coming out, Benjamin mumbled slowly, "Colvin, I ain't ungrateful or nothin' but you gotta stop drinking and turn your life to God."

"I didn't ask you for any advice," my dad snapped, but a little later Benjamin smiled to see Colvin, in his good church shirt, heading in the church's direction.

That night they came after Benjamin. Benjamin's family lived on the same farm, but in a small cabin not too far from us. Those men dragged him out of his bed. They lynched him. My father had been at the church and when he came home to see what had been done to his friend, he was heartbroken. He took the body down. The next day when he looked at the rope, he saw it was the same rope that he had used to capture that Caco, Champagne Pepla. That's when he remembered the dying man's words, 'And after me, the deluge'. He was upset that he had given those men the very tool they used to destroy his friend. Well, after months of drinking and cursing the rope, he decided to return to Haiti—to bury it."

"Those kinds of things happen in a place where the rivers flow with milk and honey?" Moiselle questioned, incredulous.

"I never saw any milk rivers. Things were hard for us. After Benjamin's death, we roamed for a bit. We were living on the coast of South Carolina when one day a ship bound for Haiti broke down. The boat had been carrying supplies for US soldiers. My father was working at the shipyard and when he found out the boat's destination, he felt it was God telling him to go to Haiti. So he offered the captain the only thing he had—his sweat in exchange for passage for the both of us to Haiti, and the captain agreed.

"When we got here, the occupation was ending. The only people who would help a poor white man and his child was the church. Priests and pastors were the only trusted white people here, so my father started preaching and pretty soon he was moving from town to town and here we are. So I guess to answer your question, I had no choice in the matter. I had to learn Kreyol to survive. You know how your father has a farm? That's your family business. My family business is preaching. We spread the good word in whatever language is needed."

"It's so sad, has he buried the rope?" Moiselle said, squeezing Robert's fingers tightly.

"No, he keeps trying to find the right place. A few times, he thought he found the right place when we were in the north, near this forest. However, he couldn't find the rope where he thought he had put it. We looked for it for days until we gave up and then, we would find it in a place where we knew we had looked. Sometimes I wonder if I dreamed the whole thing," he said. They held hands in silence for a long time. "I bet you meet lots of girls," Moiselle finally whispered. "Yes, but none of them makes me smile like you do." Moiselle followed Robert's lead and leaned into him for a deep, long kiss. He moaned as if savoring a sweet, dark grape.

The next night, Moiselle schemed how to sneak out and see Robert. He planned to meet her by the creek. She would know it was him by the soaring cricket sound he showed her. The world around was dark, the way she imagined the inside of a knapsack. She crawled out of the small opening of her hut. She had never left home this late. What if he forgot? What if he changed his mind? What if the kiss didn't mean anything to him? What if his moan was just the sign of an inexperienced man? And what if she didn't smell the goodness in his soul as she imagined she had the night before?

She was relieved when she saw him sitting at the edge of the river. She ran toward him and they hugged. "I want to take you somewhere," she said. "Promise me you are not going to stand stiffly and stand out. It's like when you invited me to church, I came and I participated." She held his hand and they ran under lazy tree branches and trampled things that squeaked as they ran through the woods. Before long they heard the thumping of the drums. Moiselle whispered, "This is like how babies know to come out into the world. This sound calling to them." He rolled his eyes, "You can be so dramatic."

In the clearing they saw about twenty men drumming. Women approached the fire pit and they moved. Several of the older, plump women lifted off the ground and twirled. "Here. Feel the rhythm." Moiselle held his palm in the air. "Clear your mind and let the rhythm guide you." Robert closed his eyes and followed Moiselle's lead. It wasn't long until his feet matched the movement of the drummer's hand. He was an instrument of rhythm. He felt himself lifted off the ground. He heard a voice say, "My sheep hear my voice." He turned to see who said it. He dropped to the ground and his body felt weighed down by an anvil. But he watched Moiselle who was flying in the air, her body a beautiful kite, cutting through dimensions, riding rhythm.

The next night, they met by the river. The light from his lantern allowed her to see in his eyes. He asked, "Is there someone whom I have to worry about if I kissed you again?"

"Too late for that."

"A man may forgive his girl one kiss, but not a second one."

"There used to be. He gave me a ring, but it's at the bottom of my well. No, you don't have to worry."

He smiled at her and in the moonlight his eyes glowed. He held his hand out. She took it. They sat in silence—her back to his chest, watching the moon and how in the short week it had grown to almost half-roundedness.

The next two days it rained, so there was no going to market for her mother and her father's friends didn't come over to play dominos. Moiselle sat anxiously counting the minutes she spent apart from Robert. Finally, three days after her meeting with Robert at the creek, her mother decided to go to the big market, as the locals called it. The smaller local market took place on Tuesdays and Thursday in Beudet, but the big market was only once a week about ten miles away in Croix des Bouquets. Moiselle loved the big market. She saw it as a spectacle, with its celebrity hagglers--vendors who controlled and flaunted their merchandise like matadors. The hagglers lay bleeding like defeated bulls, cut down by roaring laughter from crowds who came to watch rather than to buy. Come big market day in Croix des Bouquets, vendors like her mother leave their children behind and enter the open air bazaar as fiscal gladiators ready for blood.

Her mother always went to Croix des Bouquet the night before big market day. This, Moiselle knew, was a strategy that kept her at the top. By staying with her sister, Neila, who was very pregnant, her mother was sure to be rested and wake up early to be the first one to arrive at the marketplace. She always sold her produce fast and for good money, and Neila's house was a place Moiselle loved to visit. However, on this particular day Moiselle didn't volunteer to accompany her; she wanted to see Robert.

After supper that Friday, Moiselle got her father's pipe readied. He sat on the porch. His domino-playing friends arrived as soon as she brought the liquor out. It was as if they sniffed the *tafia* from their shacks. She was counting on their long, heated political discussions. At about six-thirty, as she had expected, Jean Samson arrived with a sack of sweet potatoes. He always brought something, unlike the other four men. She rolled her eyes at Jean Samson, then made a mental note at how he failed to notice her hair. Does he even know what a chignon is? He failed to notice how her skin glowed. She had spent extra time scrubbing with hibiscus and applying coconut milk to her body. Albeit for someone else, but the least he could do was to acknowledge the changes in her. How could her parents think she could marry a man like Jean Samson?

She took the sack of potatoes and signaled her little brother, Champagne, to take a seat next to her father. She had already paid him with her piece of meat from dinner. His job was to say the one name, his name, and to conjure his namesake, Champagne Pepla, who was their father's hero-saint. She knew if the men started to talk about Cacos her father would turn into emotional mush and he wouldn't notice her slipping out. The men started drinking *tafia*.

"I'm telling you," her father said, "July 28, 1915 is a date I won't ever forget. I was seventeen years old, in the middle of mango harvest. Someone rode from Port-Au-Prince to Leogane to tell us that the Americans had landed that morning. We didn't have a radio so we relied on word of mouth. It didn't take long for us to feel this occupation ...Thank you, Moiselle," her father said as she handed him more tobacco for his pipe. He slammed a *doub-sis* down, making the other dominoes jump, and in the process got rid of the old hag. His playmates winced.

"I was in the field with my four brothers, God bless their souls. Those American devils made us abandon our land and come work for the so-called national good. We were forced to clear forest to make way for roads."

At this point, Moiselle nudged her brother. "Papa, did you ever meet Champagne Pepla?"

As Moiselle expected, genuine sadness crept over her father's face. "Moiselle, bring me eh...some ...."

She handed her father the tafia.

"Son, of course I knew him—by blood we were cousins. You know that's why I named you Champagne. We were held up in the woods for about a month. Word was that the Americans had sent their best trackers to get Champagne after we blew up a ship in 1917. For almost two years we didn't rest. Champagne scattered us and we had plans to meet in one month. Champagne was a patient person; the smartest of the smart. We waited in a cave. Then, one week in 1919, it rained without stopping. Champagne left to forage for food. We always did it like that. One goes and one stays. After I noticed the shadow of the sun had moved by two hours, I became worried. I left to find him. The drizzle made it hard for me to catch his scent in the wind or his foot prints, not that he left any. He moved like a ghost in the trees. I took to the trees too. I moved from tree to tree to see if I could see him. When I saw him, he was tangled in a trap and a white man was fussing over him. I flashed him my blue handkerchief. This was our signal which meant I saw him and I was going to get help. Just as I was going to go down and fight with the white man, a bolt of lightning hit the tree I was on. I was knocked out of the tree and fell. When I came back to reality, I had a gash on my head. I had a leaf compress around my head and a nice fire was warming my body. I looked up and guess who had saved me?" Young Champagne raised his hand, begging ,"Ooh, I know, Papa, let me say the answer." His father nodded and Champagne said "It was Papa Boss. That's how you met him."

"Yes, indeed, good boy. You listen so well."

"He's only heard it a thousand times," Jean Samson joked, but the smile left his face at farmer Moises's look of disapproval.

"You said it my boy; Papa Boss was a soldier in the fight too, but we had never met before he found me almost dead in that forest. All his efforts were almost in vein because just a few months after, those devils captured me again and made me work for Mr. Chin. I, being from the north, followed Champagne to Leogane where he was in charge, and then later I joined the fight, the Cacos."

"You speak of him like he was a god?" Samson said and the other men snickered. "He was not a god, he was a saint. But on the day I was found, I looked up to see this quiet, lean giant lifting me onto his back, carrying me for miles. I couldn't even remember my name. It was months after my head injury healed and I had been living in Croix des Bouquets with his family that my life started coming back to me. But Papa Boss showed me this." He pulled out a card with a picture of the rebel leader hung and a door. "Papa Boss told me they used birds and airplanes to drop these pictures all over Haiti so that people would know that hope had died. Those monsters...those American savages killed him. Hung him to a door..." The tears began to flow. The men stopped playing dominoes and sipped some more tafia.

Moiselle took the cue, slipped quietly out the back of the property.

She found Robert waiting at the cemetery in front of a mausoleum that had no name, only a raised fishtail. It had always fascinated Moiselle, but all the people she had ever asked about it didn't know or didn't want to tell her. Some said it was an empty tomb, a sculpture like a statue. She took their word for it.

"Moiselle!" Robert hugged her.

"Have you ever seen anything like this?" Moiselle said tracing the tail. "Maybe it's a mermaid."

"It reminds me of something I saw recently--the same type of tail on a picture of a fountain they are going to build in the center of a new plaza in Port-au-Prince. Picture this big bronze sculpture with four mermaids. Some people think they are bad, that they lure men to their deaths, but I don't think so. When I was very young and was coming here on the boat, I wished to see a mermaid. Every day, when they allowed me to come up on deck, I looked out on the horizon and thought..."

"Did you see one?"

"Well, I'm looking at one magical creature now," he said, bringing his face close for a kiss. She laughed and playfully pushed him away.

"I don't think I would want to live in the ocean. I dream of being the Queen of Carnival."

Robert raised an eyebrow. "I could see that."

"I once ran away from home and got as far as Leogane—that's where I saw a real carnival. The queen wore a gorgeous yellow satin dress. It was tight right here..." she demonstrated the fitted torso. "She had a conical hat and she danced so elegantly on a white horse. You know, sometimes when I'm on my parent's mule, I pretend to be her. I sit straight like her and move the way she did."

Suddenly she slowed down because it did something to her to see how Robert sat back to watch her explain the carnival, the dancing, the costumes, and the energy. The way his eyes widened, she wondered if he wanted to freeze that moment forever.

"You're a pastor, so those things are not good for you to hear. I want to see the mermaids one day. Take me there to see them? Being stuck here, I'll never know anything about the big beautiful world out there."

Robert ran his fingers absentmindedly along her arm. The straps from her shirt came off. "Nothing is going to happen."

"You're a pastor. Aren't we supposed to do this only if we get married?" She searched his face for an answer as she unbuttoned his shirt. He unsnapped her bra and when he saw her breasts, he looked amazed. She had already thrown his belt on the ground and was pulling down his pants when she said, "Robert, if we do this, promise me you'll take me with you? Take me away from here."

He sucked in his breath and said, "Of course. I don't know what it is about you, but I know I love you. I want to marry you. That's the only reason I'm allowing myself to touch you. No, in fact you are my wife." He picked a blade of grass from the nearby tomb and fashioned a ring for her finger. Then he pulled her to him. "Let me tell the moon, the soil, and these ghosts—this is my wife, my woman."

They fell back on each other, laughing, and resumed the rapturous rhythmic exploration of each other's bodies. In the days that followed, Robert and Moiselle did a little too much dancing and not enough praying.

****

"It's a darn shame you weren't here to receive your fiancé, Robert." The voice came through the darkness as he snuck through the back gate to his room at Pastor Denis' house. Robert didn't even have to turn around to know that his father would be sitting in the moonlight, stroking his rope and talking to the moon.

"Just went for a walk and swim by the river, sir."

"That's not what I hear. If you don't want all hell and damnation on your head, you will stop swimming in that river. I won't have it." His boot against the dry floor boards echoed in the night. "Lily'll be expecting you to show her around tomorrow. So go pray whatever filth you have on you--off." Robert could not say anything, he was looking at his hands and could still feel the weight of Moiselle's breast.

Every night for two weeks Moiselle alternated between going to the river bank or the cemetery. Robert didn't show up. One morning, she went to the church, not knowing what she would say; she only knew she *had* to see him. When she got there, she asked, "Is Mrs. Pastor home?"

"No, the pastor and his wife went somewhere with all the white people," the girl said. Moiselle wondered if the girl knew something and if this is why she emphasized the word "all". This emphasis seemed to alert Moiselle not to ask about any specific white person since ALL the white people are gone. "Thank you, sister," she said, hoping the girl didn't detect the malice in her voice. She walked toward the gate to exit, but instead ran around to the side of the church. She remembered Robert telling her that he shared a room with the pastor's sons on the first floor, the last room in the back. She was happy to have remembered that detail. At the time he mentioned it, she thought nothing of it, but now it was really what she wanted. She stood on her toes and peeked in through the frosted slats of the slightly opened jalousie windows. "Robert!" she whispered emphatically, seeing him move away from the window. He then went back to the bed. "Tomorrow night by the river," she rattled quickly as she saw the servant she had spoken to approaching her. "Sister, you are lost. There are no church services this morning because the pastor and his wife..."

"..Are away with ALL the white people," Moiselle mimicked as the girl showed her the exit to the compound.

Moiselle didn't want to go home. She saw some women dressed in white head toward the Hounfort Legrand. It was the biggest voodoo compound for 20 miles. She followed them. Even if she couldn't get in, she reasoned, she could dance outside. She passed the two lions standing guard outside of the palatial estate she had admired with her bird's eye-view. She scaled the wall and danced in the shadows. Suddenly, Moiselle stopped dancing too. She saw that a group of twelve women dressed in white left the circle of dancers and entered a hut. The first was Mrs. Denis, the second her mother, and the last her mother's sister, Neila.

Inside the hut, Mrs. Denis spoke with confidence. "Cocottes, let's start our meeting. Neila, can you give us the financial report? Neila stood tall, her shadow bent by the curved roof of the hut's architecture. She said, "We've collected thirty dollars for the general funds tonight. Last year, we collected eight hundred and sent six hundred to Port au Prince. We buried the indigent widows Calvert and Germaine. We painted and repaired La siren's mausoleum. We visited our imprisoned sisters, washed, cut their hair and gave them new clothes. We bought 10 cases of dynamite and nine new guns from the Dominicans to add to our central arsenal." The women clapped at that. Neila smiled and sat back in the circle. Mrs. Denis stood again and said, "Sisters, since the days of the plantation our grandmothers' mothers met to take care of business. Our sisters in the north have been deployed into the Dominican Republic. The bad news is that a small unit of five has been captured. I'll know more in two weeks." There was a murmur of sad sighs. Mrs. Denis raised her hands, palm held midway, as if pushing back the sadness from the women. She continued, "The good news is that ships have been leaving our port filled with Syrians. The president's family has been returned to him—intact." The women clapped and her own smile seemed to elicit more claps and joyful shouts from the women. When the applause diminished, she continued, "In two months, the Cocotte of Port au Prince will use the cover of the big evangelical crusade to meet with Cocottes from all over—us included. There is much cause to wake us up. We sleep no more."

Mrs. Denis sat and someone else stood to talk. A few women had no tongues. When they opened their mouths only hollow sounds came out. Someone stood and spoke for those three women. It went down the line until everyone said something.

After the meeting was adjourned, all the women slowly headed home in pairs or other small group configurations. The Church of the Heavenly Father was less than half a mile away from Moiselle's parent's farm, the Promised Land. This being the case, it was only natural that Mrs. Moises and Mrs. Denis started to walk together. When they passed a lamp post in front of Saint Rose Catholic church. Mrs. Denis stopped and Mrs. Moises did too, each thinking the other had dropped something. Looking at the ground, searching for what she thought Mrs. Moises was searching for, Mrs. Denis said, "I know it couldn't have been easy for you seeing the young girls inducted tonight and knowing Moiselle was not chosen."

"Eveline, I'm not that selfish. She could never do the five years on the front line or stationed in the hills."

"That's true, but because of her beauty, I always thought she would be chosen and groomed to be a diplomat of a horizontal affair. It seems that those positions go to the women in Jacmel only."

"Not surprising. Our politicians love the grimels; they believe that the lightest woman is the best choice for a wife, and I bet some light-skinned politician would have loved to have Moiselle, but like we discussed at council, she would be a big risk."

The women were quiet for a minute, and then Eveline Denis said, "I see that your eye has healed well."

Mrs. Moises smiled an almost embarrassed smile and said, "You know for some reason, after the night my husband received a visit from the Cocottes he has stopped hitting me."

Eveline Denis cackled, "That's something that should have been done a long time ago. The nerve of him! All of his professed love for Champagne Pepla. And he would hit you, knowing Champagne was the love of your life and you his."

"Eveline, you're trying to flatter me," Mrs. Moises said, pausing to look longingly at the half moon. "I hope I was the love of Champagne's life. I certainly loved him like I have never loved any other man. For a long time, I thought Moises' hitting me was what I deserved for refusing to kill the child of my rapist."

"Come on now, Poupette," Eveline Denis's eyes narrowed. Poupette Moises's lips quivered. Then, Eveline's voice softened. "Since the day Papa Boss brought your tortured body back from that battlefield—that forest—I knew you were meant to survive. When it became clear that you were pregnant, I prayed you would keep it. I wanted to believe that the real reason you kept Moiselle is the possibility that she could be Champagne's too, right?" Poupette bobbed her head. A tear dripped from her eyes and traveled down the vertical part of a cross etched on her nose. Eveline pulled out a handkerchief from her dress and gave it to Poupette. In the distance, as if on cue, a dog howled non-stop. "Don't ever forget that hopeful possibility, because you told me yourself you were with him for three days before that animal attacked you."

Poupette nodded her head up and down again, and took a breath to say, "That's true. But you know, for the life of me, I don't know why I ever told Moises about the rape. It seemed it would have been easier on me and on her if he believed for the rest of his life that Moiselle was Champagne's child. You know he beats her now."

Eveline chuckled, "That son of a bitch. Well, I hear it's only when he can catch her. I hear he can get one or two good licks in and after that he can't catch her. Maybe we can ask the saints to come out of hiding and kidnap him again, tie him up, and dip his balls in honey and have some red ants have at him again."

Poupette doubled over with laughter, then as they resumed their leisurely pace, she said, "Oh, when they brought him back home that time last year, he almost died from an infection in his balls. He deserved it for hitting me, but you know she is sixteen; she has to get married this year or else she is going to ruin herself the way she and that white boy go after each other."

Eveline picked leaves from a soursop tree they passed and then she said, "So you've seen him."

"Yes, New Year's eve, I saw him leaving the farm. He tipped his hat at me and then stood there looking at me like he had been hit by lightning."

"Poupette, I've been wrestling with whether to tell you this for a couple of weeks now. The Beast-of-a-kingdom-past is here in Croix des Bouquets."

Poupette stopped, turned, and pulled at Eveline's arms in disbelief. Then, she squatted and placed her head between her knees. Eveline crouched next to her, stroking her head. A few minutes later, Poupette said, "I'm sorry. That news hit me in the gut and I felt I was going to faint or vomit."

Eveline said, "I would not have believed it, but right at my dinner table, he tells the story of capturing Champagne and of branding Champagne's female werewolf lover." Poupette collapsed on the dirt floor and sat with her white dress covering her knees, leaving her swollen ankles exposed. Crickets in nearby bushes reminded them to start talking again. Poupette said, "Maybe you're right. I was meant to live. You know he left me there to die. He cut off my face. Turned off the fire. Left me bound. Later, someone came on a horse. He got off and the horse wandered to where I was. At first, I thought it was the animal who had returned to finish me off.

I screamed and a man came. Even though blood covered my eyes, when he brought his torch near me, I could see he was an American soldier. 'You're going to be alright he kept saying in bad Kreyol. An animal must have attacked, you ma'am.' As the man spoke, I passed out, but I came in and out and each time he said, I'm Jake and I'm not going to hurt you. He built a fire and placed me next to it. I've gotta get help, he kept saying. If I put you on my horse, you might have permanent bone deformations. Before I passed out for the last time that evening, he told me the fire should last until he returned and he would be back with a few men to carry me down the mountain and take me to a doctor. Then, five minutes later, I heard an explosion and screams and I never heard him again. Two days later, it was Papa Boss Dubin who found me. He brought me here to Croix des Bouquets where he had also brought Moises, also injured, also found in that forest. You know the rest."

Eveline rubbed Poupette's shoulder gently as she said, "Fear is a demon. Try not to let it in. His name is Colvin Donner, did you know that?" Poupette shook her head from left to right. Then, both women were silent—as if each one was shoveling through the deepest tar pit inside their mind. "How is he staying at your house?" There was an accusation of betrayal in her tone. "Well, apparently, he is the senior director of missions for the denomination Daniel has the church covered under. If we stay under their denomination, they give Daniel a salary from America. $1500 a year. You see why I put up with their white nonsense."

"I want to kill him myself. Eveline, you must promise me you will arrange for me to kill him."

"Okay. They're leaving in two weeks. On Saturday night, I'm going to have my husband take the son, Robert, to pray at the asylum. I will put something in Colvin's dinner so he will sleep."

"Not too much. I want him to feel my knife when I slice his balls off."

Eveline cringed. "Okay. Spare me the details. What will we tell Robert? He will want revenge. What of his feelings for Moiselle?"

Poupette smiled, "His realizing that I killed his father will be a good way to get Moiselle away from his grasps. He will kill me or try to and she will hate him." Eveline patted Poupette on the back. "I love the way this plan is shaping up."

By this point of the conversation, the women had reached the church gate and neither Eveline nor Poupette were surprised to see Farmer Moises waiting there. He held a woman's sweater in his hand. His shirt was buttoned up. Moises's hat had wafted too many fires, the proof was stamped along the edges of his hat. "I came to walk you home, Poupette," he said, not looking at Eveline. Eveline walked around him, pulled Poupette a few feet away and whispered in her ear, "If the plan changes, I'll send a girl with a red cloth."

A few days later, Poupette was fanning the fire under a pot when a young girl appeared outside of the Promised Land's gate. The girl held the red piece of cloth up until Poupette acknowledged the message by waving a hand. Immediately, she threw some water over the open flame. The young girl went back towards the church, and Poupette went in the opposite direction toward the banana plantation near Hounfort Legrand.

"Poupette, over here." She looked through a throng of banana laden trees to see Eveline Denis. Poupette whispered, "I got your message. What happened?"

"Our plan has been ruined." She paused, searching Poupette's face for a reaction. "The old man attacked a maid. He beat her pretty badly. Now, the maid's brothers have vowed to return tomorrow to cut him up. The son, Robert, is packing up and they're going away today."

"Champagne, you abandoned me in this world; naked without your love. Where is my vengeance from this scourge?" Poupette sobbed to the wind, suddenly not caring who heard her. Eveline pulled her into the trees, and wiped the tears streaming down her face. Eveline wrapped her arms around her friend's shoulder. "Poupette, keep it together. There will be other chances. The time might not be now." Eveline held Poupette, trying to calm the rage that was trying to break free.

****

It had been a few days since Moiselle had seen her mother, aunt, and Mrs. Denis at the Hounfort. She questioned how her protestant family friend, Mrs. Denis, could be at a voodoo ceremony. She felt like everyone around her were hypocrites. She thought back to Mrs. Denis' lecture about letting God choose the right man for you. *What a hypocrite!* She wanted to talk about it with Robert. But he had not come to the river for almost a week.

One night, when the moon had reached its pregnant-roundedness, Moiselle again went to meet Robert by the river. She waited and when he finally came, she was trembling with relief.

"I thought you weren't coming," she accused.

"It was difficult to leave. All week long and every night when I try to sneak out, my dad always has something for me to do. We've been found out. Someone saw us in this very spot."

"So what?" she said, standing on her toe to kiss his nose as she liked to do.

He pushed her away, gently. "No. we can't continue."

"You promised me that if we did what we did, you'd marry me and take me with you."

He was silent, rubbing his hands over his head.

"You men are all the same. You take and promise and break your promise. So you came to tell me you're leaving and that your daddy doesn't want you to have a stupid, backward black wife, is that it?" she said, shoving him in the chest.

"It's not only that. There's more" he quickly realized the effect of his words and said, "You can never be backward." He paused and when she didn't look at him, he continued, "We have to leave because my dad confronted a maid whom he suspected was trying to kill him—he thought she was poisoning him. He's suspected her for a while now. Two nights ago, I was coming here, but something told me to go back and check up on him. That's when it all happened. Now, her brothers are threatening to come and cut us up with machetes." Moiselle didn't say a thing. She wondered why she hadn't heard of this. She began to walk away. He lunged after her. He missed a step and fell back. He stayed down. Gently, he grabbed her ankle and she fell on him.

It was a soft kiss that she didn't resist. "I'm not saying it's over. I'm just asking for time to get him to safety and get him used to the idea of us," he whispered.

Knowing what she already knew about the moon's fullness and her not shedding her blood during the growth of the moon, she let his passion wash over her. In the few times they were together, she had prayed to get pregnant so he would be forced to marry her in a church. A similar thing had happened to a second cousin in Port-au-Prince. But now, she regretted that prayer because the revival was over and the caravan was moving on to an undisclosed location, without her.

The moon had shed its baby weight and was thin again, looking to feed on human admiration. Moiselle looked at it and wondered if there was a way to cancel her answered prayer. She was replaying Robert's fervent promise to return after she had hurled her dinner behind the mud-hut, when her mother came outside to stand by her side.

"Well, you have finally done it," she said. "Who is the father?"

Moiselle didn't answer.

"You better go to your aunt Neila's house tomorrow. That's the only place your father won't go to kill you. Better thank God for Papa Boss."

This wasn't the reaction she expected from her mother. She didn't expect understanding—duplicity even. She whispered, "Thank you."

"I hope he was worth ruining your life."

"Mom, this boy is a preacher. He is going to marry me when he comes back; he spread fire at the pulpit and awakened my soul. Watch, he is going to take me away from this place."

"Oh, that white man I saw walking up the road that New Year's Eve?" her mother mumbled as a faraway look crossed her face. It was a face Moiselle recognized as her addition face—when she was adding up the clues on who stole from her and who hadn't paid her at the market place. Moiselle's mother squeezed her shoulder, shook her head, and went back inside.

Moiselle didn't wait for the morning; she walked to her aunt Neila's house under the protection of darkness, the moon complicit. Moiselle saw the path and a sudden calm took over. She wasn't scared of the rustling bushes or the strange shadows of natural or unnatural things. Before she knew it, she had arrived at her destination, but it was still dark. The chairs that should be on the porch had been taken inside, as is the custom. So, she slept standing with her head leaning against the wall of her aunt's house. She knew better than to knock; country folks believed only a devil thumped at a door at night, so they never answered.

When the sun came up, Papa Boss was the first to open the door. He stood on the porch and threw kisses at the sky. Upon seeing Moiselle waiting outside of his door, he said nothing. Another lean frame slipped through the open door quietly. Moiselle was happy to see her aunt.

"My mother said I should come and live with you and Papa Boss for a while," she said.

"Will I get the full story from you or should I wait to see her come market day?" Aunt Neila inquired.

Aunt Neila was almost as tall as her husband, with a protruding stomach and long, braided, soft-to-the touch cotton hair. Moiselle always admired how gently she moved and the way her shoulders stayed back as if her breasts were propped up on a platter. Aunt Neila had not gained any weight during her pregnancies with Moiselle's two little cousins, Phillippe and Victor. Looking at her aunt's belly now, she touched her own stomach and a secret warmth spread in her heart.

"Well, make yourself useful." Papa Boss handed her a broom to sweep the front porch. She watched him place his hoe over his shoulder, a beat-up straw hat on his head, and his pipe in his mouth. He waved goodbye as he headed towards the acres he farmed a couple of miles away.

She started sweeping the porch; she knew the routine because everyone did it in the morning. *Sweep away the night. The secrets. The dead dreams.* Then she retrieved water from the well and sprinkled water over the brown earth to keep it from escaping with the wind. She rested a bit after tidying the front yard. She wondered where Robert was at that very moment, what he was doing.

"Try this old dress on and then come help me skin the goat. Keep the one you came in on the hook for Sunday mass," Aunt Neila said, interrupting her thoughts.

As the days passed, Moiselle was engulfed in this quiet rhythm between the two adults. Moiselle didn't remember ever hearing her aunt and uncle speak rudely to each other or argue. They seemed to have their own language. They worked well, like lyric and melody. But Moiselle was still not calm. Every shadow behind the trees or the outhouse was her father waiting to thrash her. She dreamed that he ripped this blan's baby out of her and spat on it.

Beudet, located in the middle of the plains, tilted between modern and old-fashioned values. Moiselle wondered what made people like Robert think this little place was different from many other little places. Was it the flatness of the region's terrain in a land of mountains? Was it the greenness peppered by huts or modest houses? It was close enough to Port-au-Prince to accept certain things, but people still believed that a girl should remain a virgin until she was married. So when word spread—and it did—people gave Moiselle the stare. Then the visits started to come. A month after moving in with her aunt, while she was still in her first trimester, Marie Maude came. She liked to call herself assistant to Mr. Chin, but everyone knew that she cleaned his house. Marie Maude often reminded anyone listening that she spoke Spanish, French, and English, but in the company of natives of those languages she seemed to only be able to recall Kreyol.

Her laughter penetrated the thin walls that separated the bedrooms from the living room, waking Moiselle from a light sleep. She could picture Marie Maude with a raised skin tag on the outside of her left eye, her hair in a tight bun, wearing dresses that were always too tight for her, talking to Aunt Neila.

"Cousin Neila, pregnancy agrees with you. I hope this is a girl. Those two boys deserve a sister." There was more laughter, and Moiselle pictured Marie-Maude touching Aunt Neila's stomach. People got so much amusement out of that. Was that going to happen to her too? "More seriously though, I've heard the news. We can't let her walk around during the day. You need to keep her inside. Right now they are just rumors, but if no one sees her, the tongues will stop wagging and if she sends the child to Port-au-Prince to the nunnery, no one will ever know."

Moiselle sat up. She hadn't thought about that. She had never considered that her family might make her give the baby away. Suddenly she wanted to protect the baby from everyone.

Aunt Neila said, "Interested in some sweet potato pudding pie? Moiselle made it yesterday. You know how good she is. Try some with some of this cremas that Papa Boss made. Tell me if you taste the rum."

Marie Maude's silence indicated that she was enjoying the rum in the cremas and the sweet potato pudding. After about five minutes, she resumed. "Do you know the father? The child, I hear, is from a white man. It's going to be beautiful. Many of the rich light skinned people will gladly take it. Talk to her. Don't let her think she's going to walk around and put ideas into the minds of the other young girls. You know how the saying goes, monkeys sees monkeys do."

"Marie-Maude, I can't possibly keep her in this hot house all day."

"Let her wet her dress and sit by the window, but people shouldn't see her. Oh, before I forget, this is a basket of little clothes and they are in good condition for her baby. I stopped by all the cousins in Thomazeau and Mireballais and they sent a few things thinking they were for you. I can imagine how much of a burden an extra mouth must be. But thank God she's got you because I can see her crazy-as-a-rabid-dog father slipping a noose around her neck before giving her money for a white man's baby."

"These are really lovely, Marie-Maude."

"This one is from Cousin Nicole, you should see her kids—tall now like palm trees. Oh, this is from Jumelle, oh no, Clemente didn't send anything. Her kids are destructive and she can never save any of their clothes." She went on and on, until the heat overtook

Moiselle who fell into a dream where a noose at the end of a rope chased her.

The sun was entangled in a distant mesh of blueness when Papa Boss's nephew, Jean-Charles, came galloping on a borrowed horse to proclaim terrible news. The young boy, his drenched shirt cuffed at the elbows and with chest heaving, didn't even get off the horse —he had other relatives as far as Thomazeau to alert. "My father is dead," he said.

Papa Boss held onto the post of the veranda; it was the first time Moiselle had ever seen him shaken. He fixed his eyes at Jean-Charles and Moiselle wondered if Papa Boss thought he heard it correctly. "But how?" is all he managed to say.

"After a cock fight." Jean-Charles looked down towards the horse's hoof, as if he could find the story of a more dignified way to die by looking at the dirt.

Aunt Neila rushed and wrapped her arms around her husband while Moiselle joined her in helping him into a seat. "How's your mother taking it?" Aunt Neila asked, as Papa Boss seemed lost for words.

"She's scared. She told me to go tell Dad's brothers to come to the house so we can plan the funeral."

"Go safely, Jean-Charles, we'll be there in the morning before the sun gets comfortable in the sky."

They watched as Jean-Charles and the horse became a spec in the distance. Then Papa Boss, patting his wife's hand said, "Excuse me ladies."

When Papa Boss was inside the bedroom, Aunt Neila was the first to talk. "This is a burden that has fallen on us. Joachim probably lost all his money in the fight."

"What are you going to do?" Moiselle asked, suddenly feeling like her aunt's joy was her only concern. "We are going to have to tie a rope around our waist for strength. And then I'm going to ask each of my sisters and cousins to reach deep into their bras and help out."

Moiselle marveled as her aunt went on about the ceremonies and formalities that needed to be performed in a week, a day, an hour, a minute—she laid out a mile's worth of plans.

Moiselle welcomed the chore of taking care of her little cousins while her aunt and uncle went to Bon Repos where Joachim's farm is located. When they returned, he went to bed again and her aunt informed her, "The funeral is this Saturday. How are you feeling, because I'm going to need your help? Joachim's wife wants a voodoo burial and your uncle wants no part of that. So we'll have a little reception and the wake for his brother here on Friday."

Moiselle liked the sound of that; it didn't even bother her that they only had three days to prepare. Even though a wake was somber, it was going to be a lot happier than being stuck with the two quietest people in the world.

People started to arrive on Friday afternoon as the sun was setting. Moiselle wore a black dress that hid the little pouch forming at the base of her stomach. Rows of borrowed wooden benches encircled the fire pit, and three shadows distorted by the dancing flames scared the little children. The smell of rum, cinnamon, and ginger permeated the yard. Steady drum beats called to neighbors far and near.

Every time Moiselle entered the kitchen, her aunt handed her a tray with something to distribute to the growing crowd. The marriage of well-marinated chicken strips dipped into a batter of crushed parsley appealed to her, but as soon as she placed it in her mouth, she had to drop the tray and run to the outhouse. Everything she consumed that day came out of her like a cat choking on hairballs, although she managed to distribute several rounds of *tafia* and ginger tea. After, she stood watching the town's crier. Calico was a short man with the complexion of a carrot, hired to get people crying or laughing, depending on the circumstances surrounding the death. As Joachim had been stabbed after a cock fight, Calico began with wails capable of reaching the realm of the dead. She felt the heavy breath of a whisper on her neck and turned to see Jean-Pierre's crooked teeth smiling at her. "Well, if it isn't the self-proclaimed healer and musician," she said then added, "Don't you have some priest to drive around?"

"Moiselle, Moiselle, Moiselle. I saw you and Pastor Robert pray by the river a few months ago. I love the way you pray," he said slyly and Moiselle wouldn't have reacted differently had he walked up to her and slapped her in the face. "You should know, didn't the priest teach you to pray?" A vein popped out on Jean-Pierre's forehead. "Moiselle, you have a dirty mind and a dirty mouth. No wonder Pastor Robert chose the white lady over you."

Jean-Pierre doubled over in laughter at the shocked look on her face. "I'm going to forget that you just insulted me and do something nice for you. See how nice I am. I brought you her picture to show you." Jean-Pierre held it out. Moiselle stared at the composed young woman with the blonde curls cascading around her shoulders. The hurt was too raw for her to keep her composure. She leaned against the wall and slid to the floor in an ungraceful squat.

"I know what you're hinting at, but there is nothing that says she is anything to him." Moiselle reached again for the picture and thought the lace on her blouse was very common. It's the kind of lace available at the big market.

"I picked her up from the docks myself. They're probably married by now," he said, shaking his head.

"Moiselle, where have you---oh Jean-Pierre, how are you? For a minute I didn't notice you standing there. I thought Moiselle had fallen down," Aunt Neila said as she helped Moiselle to her feet. "I'm doing well, Madan Boss," Jean-Pierre volunteered, his voice steady and clear like an altar boy. Moiselle turned away without saying anything to Jean-Pierre.

As Aunt Neila loaded more food on her serving tray, Moiselle's mind raced. *Was he right? Did Robert really marry someone else without telling me? What about our love? What about his proclamation of marriage by the river?* She decided if Jean-Pierre came near her, she'd say in her coldest voice, "Well, good for Robert. I got what I wanted from him and sent him on his way." Or maybe she would look Jean-Pierre in the eyes, put her hand on her hip, and say, "Why would I want to marry that broke preacher? Don't you know Samson has asked me to marry him, and you know how much land Samson has?" She decided to go with the latter scenario. She rehearsed it in her mind, but instead of approaching her, Jean-Pierre sat behind the bongos, drumming. Each time their eyes met, he threw his head back and laughed.

Her back started to ache, so she headed to the corner of the yard where the fire pit blazed. Marie-Maude and her aunt were engaged in conversation with two neighbors whom Moiselle had seen but hadn't really talked to. Moiselle took off her shoes, and the rotund woman dressed in blue scrunched her face and said, "Foreign shoes. White shoes--- they'll mess you up every time." The two women laughed. When Moiselle saw the embarrassed look on Aunt Neila's face, she knew that everyone knew what had happened between her and Robert. Before she could put her shoes back on, Marie-Maude said, "Go to sleep, Moiselle, can't you see grown women are talking. You are a child."

The other two women burst out laughing, "Oh Marie-Maude, you're too funny. Let the girl stay; she probably knows more than we do. The milk has spilled," the women cackled.

Her aunt was silent as Marie-Maude poked at the glowing coals in the pit. Moiselle looked back a couple of times; in the somber light of the flickering flames from the fire pit, her aunt's anger and disappointment was abundantly clear to her. Her head flopped down; she thought her face was going to touch the brownish soil.

Moiselle was grateful for her aunt and uncle's silence; it allowed her every thought to be on Robert Donner—where was he? What was he doing? Did he really marry the white woman in that picture? Did he know the woman before he met her? Did she know his God? Is that what I've done wrong, not believing enough like Pastor Denis' wife had warned me to do? If he was with this woman, did he touch her the way he touched Moiselle? Some mornings that last question bound her hand, foot, mind, and heart so badly that she could not roll out of bed. She was stiff with self-doubt—as if someone had pumped cement into her veins. She resented her tears—that they were not enough to fill the room and drown her.

She didn't have to be told by her aunt to stay inside—away from judgmental eyes. She elected to wet her two dresses and sat inside the house. On the rare day she didn't wake up thinking about Robert being with another woman, she mended and altered the baby clothes that Marie-Maude had brought. She made new ones out of scraps. She embroidered flowers on the clothes, then she took them out, thinking the baby might be a boy.

One day, Moiselle was sitting under the open window of her room. Her aunt approached her, wiping her face? With a grand gesture meant to be funny. "One day when I'm a rich woman," Aunt Neila said, fanning herself with her straw hat. Moiselle laughed, "You would still live like a poor woman." Aunt Neila squeezed and pulled Moiselle's braids playfully, "Let me help you embroider." Her aunt plopped down and grabbed a pink cloth and started to thread a needle. Once the needle received its thread, she started to whistle a song, *"Ti poulet souve, wi wa.."* Moiselle joined her in the silly Kreyol children's nursery rhyme about an escaped little chicken who must be captured to make chicken soup for the queen.

The more Moiselle sang it, the more she felt like she was the chick. A tear escaped her.

"I didn't mean to make you sad," Aunt Neila said softly. "I thought the little song and company would cheer you up. I remember how, when you were little, you used to run around in that circle with your cousins singing that song. You were a fast little chicken and no one could catch you," she laughed.

Moiselle wiped her tear. "It's just that you and Papa Boss never get mad or say anything to me about what I've done. Then you come to sing this song and I get to thinking maybe you're trying to tell me something. Maybe you're trying to tell me that I'm the little run away chick."

Aunt Neila held Moiselle's chin gently. "Of course we would have loved to see you wait and marry before having a baby, but it's not for us to judge. The Lord is allowing it for a reason. I think of so many women who want children, but can't have them—like Marie-Maude for example. God must have a plan." Then, she got up from the small rattan chair, and squeezed Moiselle's hand as she left the room. Moiselle could hear her whistle that song as she started the afternoon meal.

Nights were not any better. She heard Robert's voice clearly in her dreams. Often, she spoke to him in dreams; his voice, like the luring trumpet of mermaids, called her to windows and made her walk outside of the house. "Wake up, Moiselle," Papa Boss said one night, nudging her gently back into the house. "This is the fifth time tonight, Neila. I'm going to go through the window and block the door from the outside and then I'll climb back in."

Moiselle was unaware of her aunt putting her back in her bed. She repeated in a trance, "I'm your wife. You told the moon and the ghosts, Robert."

A few weeks later, while she was sitting in her room looking through the small window, she noticed two feet lying on the ground outside. Immediately, she knew they belonged to her aunt, who had gone outside to prepare the mid-day meal. Did she faint? Had she fallen? Papa Boss was out working on the farm and their two sons were at school. What could she do? She waddled outside to find, indeed, Aunt Neila panting and moaning softly.

"Contractions, child."

"Don't say that Auntie, you can't be having the baby now. I'm all alone with you."

Aunt Neila huffed and squeezed Moiselle's hand for what seemed like an eternity. "Help me to my bed. Take the horse to the neighbor and have them fetch Piti, the midwife."

Moiselle moved faster than she thought her six-month-old pregnant belly should allow. She ran to the pasture where the horse grazed. She stopped twice to catch her breath. She approached the horse slowly like she had seen Papa Boss do, and then she walked with it at a brisk pace to the neighbor's house. Once there, she called, "Honor!" and a short, round-faced woman appeared. "Auntie," she called, even though the woman wasn't her aunt and had insulted her and called her spilled milk. The neighbor stared at her belly and contorted her face. Moiselle ignored this and said, "Madan Papa Boss is in labor. She sent this horse so your son can get Piti faster."

The neighbor motioned for her son who quickly volunteered to retrieve Piti. "You tell your aunt I'll be over to help after the baby is born, but right now I have to tend to my sick mother."

When Moiselle returned to the house, Aunt Neila was still moaning. "Did the boy go?" she said between gritted teeth. "Yes. His mother said she'll come by after the baby is born. Apparently, she's taking care of her mother." She could tell a contraction had ended because Aunt Neila glowed with relief. "Is that what that old witch is using as an excuse? You know she's a werewolf and can't help herself around babies." "Auntie that's a rumor," Moiselle stressed the last syllable, her eyes wide open. "That boy is the only baby who survived. She had twelve others besides him; she had eaten each of her babies." Moiselle had never heard her aunt carry on like that about others, but since it kept the pain at bay, she was willing to go along with it. "Whose other children has she eaten? No wonder she's so fat?" "Marie-Maude suspects that she's got something to do with her miscarriages," Moiselle listened as she fetched the wood from the pile on the porch that Papa Boss had cut that morning. She propped the back door so that wind circulated from the front and penetrated the house. She made a fire and began to boil water as Aunt Neila counted the numbers of mysterious baby deaths attributed to the round-faced neighbor.

"I wish Phillippe and Victor hadn't gone to the farm with Papa Boss," Moiselle said nervously after the stories had stopped, trying to make conversation to keep her aunt's mind off of her pain. As soon as she was done she returned to the room, relieved that Piti had arrived.

"Madan Boss, it's a good day to have a baby!" Piti exclaimed, her round body shaking in laughter. "The young man who came to retrieve me told me to let you know he is taking the horse so he can go fetch Papa Boss." She signaled for Moiselle to give her a helping hand while, effortlessly, she propped Aunt Neila into a squatting position between two chairs. She tested the water to see how hot it was. She began to massage Aunt Neila and to sing songs. "I'm calling the ancestors to make a clear path for the baby," she said.

Aunt Neila was too tired to fight or to make requests. She hung on to those two chairs like a climber hangs on to a cliff. Moiselle's job was to hold her aunt's head and shoulders. She wiped her face with a wet cloth. Each scream, each moan of pain sent Moiselle into a hole of fear. She wondered about her own turn, her own pain. She knew she couldn't get out of having the baby; it was like being carried away by a river, a river of time and circumstance. Where could she find a tree branch to hold on to?

A small vulnerable human being was born three hours later. Piti and Moiselle helped Neila to her bed. "Madan Boss, your babies always come so fast. You are blessed. Some women spend hours and even days in labor," Piti commented as she cleaned the baby. "I'm only sorry that Papa Boss missed it," Moiselle said so softly the other two women gave no indication of hearing it. After, Piti handed her the baby. Aunt Neila whispered some sweet cooing words to the baby and then said to Moiselle, "Go ahead, hold her. Meet your cousin, Charlotte."

Moiselle sat next to her aunt on the bed. She held the baby in her arms while her aunt slept and Piti tidied up. For so long now, Moiselle had felt like she was drowning in a turbulent river, but looking at Charlotte, the river was calm and she was floating. She marveled at the tiny brown hairs on the pale skin. She smelled the tiny fingers with the brown coloring inching from the cuticles—a sign of the color to come later. Moiselle wondered if her baby would be born pale like Charlotte: would she turn out a rich brown or stay Robert's color? Moiselle remembered the first time she knew that people came in different colors. She and her mother had been sitting by the river, washing clothes. She was five. A man came on a brown horse. While his horse drank water, he filled a thermos. Moiselle fell in the river when the man said, "Honor" in Kreyol.

"It is rude to stare, pretty girl," he continued as he reached to help her get out of the river. "They call me Doc down in Croix des Bouquets," the man offered. Words were not coming out of Moiselle's open mouth. Her mother grabbed her away from Doc with a quickness and stood behind her with one arm across Moiselle's torso. She breathed hard.

"I mean no harm, madam. Just giving my horse some water, saw that your daughter had fallen in and I was helping her out" Doc explained. It wasn't until the man's back was to them and he had disappeared into the bushes that Moiselle noticed that her mother held a big knife behind her back.

Moiselle asked, "Manman, why did that white man scare you?" Her mother didn't respond. She continued to beat the bedsheets she was washing. "Manman, how do some people get to be white and some black like us?" Moiselle continued with the questions.

Her mother turned to look at her for a long minute. "Zel, stop flapping." Wings stop beating. This was a play on her nick-name

Zel. At any other time, she would smile, but she was curious and wanted answers. "Manman, please tell me," she persisted.

Her mother grabbed her chin and looked at her pointedly. "Look at the bottom of your feet, what do you see?" Moiselle looked. "It's white," Moiselle said, innocently.

"Well, that should tell you something. There is nothing to be impressed about whiteness or light-skinned people. The color white is meant to be trampled on. This is why God made the soles of all feet white."

Moiselle thought all that afternoon and most of her life until now about it. Now, sitting here wondering if her baby would be white like Robert or black like her, she realized her mother was wrong. Moiselle couldn't think of one white or light skinned person who was ever in an inferior position. They always seemed, like the woman on her balcony sipping wine, to be better off than all the people with her skin color. She thought very hard about this. All the hard-working people like Papa Boss or her father seem to be running in place. Maybe her mother was wrong; maybe God meant to give humanity black soles, but He ran out of ink.

Moiselle smelled Charlotte's pristine breath. She hoped her baby would be Robert's color or close to it. Suddenly, for the first time, she knew the four months she had left could not come fast enough. The river inside her was calm.

In the weeks that followed, Moiselle didn't mind staying inside the house to watch over the baby. Sometimes she had to fight, playfully, with Phillippe and Victor. "My turn, my turn to hold her," they shouted. They brought their games of kicking a ball back and forth closer to the house so they could be near the baby. They grudgingly went to school and kissed her many times before leaving. Every hour it seemed another relative from far or near dropped by to see the baby.

What Moiselle hated about those visits were the stares. Sometimes she retreated to her room, her eyes to the floor, not challenging any adult by being there.

A few weeks after Charlotte's birth, Moiselle's mother walked through the doors. Moiselle felt weak in the knees. She hadn't realized how much she had missed seeing her mother. She thought she was strong, a grown woman now that she was going to be a mother. Her mother only squeezed her hand and called to her in that special soft tone, "Zel, you flying or resting?" Moiselle wondered if her mother didn't want to hug her for fear that other relatives might think she condoned her pregnancy. "Manman, how is market going?" Moiselle asked, but the other woman raised their voices in discussion to drown her out. Moiselle scanned their faces. She realized that all twelve women present had head wraps the color of blood. She realized it had been a long time since a girl had been born in the family. For a moment a twinge of jealousy and fear fell over her that if she had a daughter, her daughter would not receive such subtle, poetic acknowledgements. "Manman, has Champagne asked for me?" Moiselle asked, but her mother had turned her back to her and was cooing at the baby. Had she misunderstood the touch of the warm, weather-worn hands that touched her face when she entered the house? Moiselle closed her eyes, thinking about how those hands had washed her face, combed her hair, and nursed her from fevers all her life. She understood that the women wanted her to be quiet. Was she a reminder of how hopes can go wrong? Was she a reminder of how much hard work can go wrong? She sat on a chair in the corner watching her mother with the baby. She wondered if her mother would come to see her baby. She knew her father wouldn't let her.

Her mother took off her head wrap; something she rarely did in public. She wiped the sweat pouring from her head to her face with the red cloth. Then, she fanned Charlotte with her wrap. At once Moiselle saw and remembered the cross scarred on her mother's face. Usually, her mother wears a scarf worn so low that the scar is not visible. Its vertical leg ended at the tip of her nose and its arms touched both of her eyes. Moiselle also looked at her aunts and cousin and took in a breath. She never realized that they were all crossed. Her cousins and aunts from Beudet had crosses on their left shoulders. Only her mother and her aunt Neila had crosses on their noses. Aunt Neila's was very small—hardly visible and closer to her eyebrow. Then, she realized something. She wondered what ritual she had escaped. She wondered if this was some weird fashion of the past---like piercing ears. See it's this sort of thing that makes me want to leave Croix des Bouquets, she thought. Then, she reasoned, I supposed it's no different than people putting two holes in their ears. Maybe crossing on the nose wasn't so weird.

"Look at those plum lips, just like Moiselle," her mom said and everyone turned to look at Moiselle. The sentence was a match her mother had not intended to strike. The frozen terrified reaction of the people sitting in the living room told Moiselle that they hoped that the baby's plum lips wouldn't lead her to end up pregnant and abandoned at sixteen. The river of panic grabbed her again and she didn't excuse herself when she left for her room.

Later, as fewer relatives came, Moiselle came out of her room to hold the baby more often. "Moiselle, put that baby down before you spoil her," her aunt and uncle would say. "What are you going to do when your baby comes? Charlotte is going to be so jealous."

After dinner Moiselle would go outside so Papa Boss could have time in his house without being reminded of her presence. He had not said anything to make her feel unwelcome. In fact, he didn't seem to mind her being there. However, there was something inside of her that told her she should give him space or the right to resent her—even though he hadn't asked for it.

Despite her fears of her father and the prying stares of strangers, she mustered the courage every night, month after month, to walk to the cemetery to visit the mermaid tomb. *Mermaid, mermaid, I'm throwing all tears back to you. Take them to the sea.* "Mermaid, do you remember the time Robert kissed me right here?" The grass still felt soft, the jasmine still sent out its heavenly scent. The only thing missing was the indigo sky and the stars—somehow her sky had changed. "God, if you bring him back, I promise to be good.

I'll stop dancing, stay away from the drums, and I'll go to church with Robert. Just make him come back, please," she bargained, her forehead leaning on the mermaid's empty tomb.

Crickets hummed so loudly that the drums in the distance were an afterthought. After the moon had shown seven full pregnant bellies to Moiselle, she gained new hope. She looked at the moon and envied it. *Where do you put your babies? Every month pregnant with so much light, only to face the world as a sliver of a thing.* Her head was heavy with bad thoughts. They piled on top of her like the stale wares of an inexperienced peddler. The river of doubt and panic was raging inside of her again. She thought about leaving the baby in the woods or drowning it. She wanted to be skinny like a thirty-two-day-old moon and run away to somewhere new. The next minute, she felt bad about those thoughts and felt deserving of abandonment.

One night, as she climbed down the little hillock from the cemetery, she felt her first contraction. She moaned, turning from the moon. *God, are you watching?* She fell to her knees, riddled with pains in her abdomen and lower back. Her second contraction didn't hit her until she reached her aunt's house. The pain in her back felt like the pummeling of coconuts; she walked on all fours to the living room where she collapsed.

When Aunt Neila heard Moiselle's cries, she came out, placed the lantern on the floor, and said, "Sweetheart, how many sharp pains have you had?"

"Just two. Sorry, I think I peed on myself."

Neila felt around her bottom and inner thigh. "Judging on how wet your dress is, your water broke not too long ago."

Papa Boss nodded, put on his hat and left the house to get Piti.

A rivulet of sweat ran from her forehead, down the valley of her breasts. "She's got a long way to go," Piti said, looking up from where she squatted between Moiselle's legs, poking, measuring and feeling the textures of the liquids coming out of her. "Guess who else has two other ladies in labor tonight?" "No, you don't say!" Aunt Neila exclaimed. "I have a feeling Moiselle's baby is going to take a little bit of time, so I'm going to go check on the two other ladies down the street and I'll come back in a couple of hours." "What do I do if the baby comes?" Aunt Neila asked, panic written all over her face. "It's not going to come in two hours. We'll be lucky if it comes in fifteen. So while I'm gone, walk around with her. Hold her up under one arm and have Papa Boss do the same with the other arm."

"Okay, let's go, you heard Piti," Aunt Neila said, wrapping one of Moiselle's arms around her neck as Papa Boss did the same. Another contraction sliced through her. Moiselle was sure she was no longer one person and no amount of glue would put her back together. "Okay, it's going away. Breathe through your nose; it will help." Moiselle trembled and moaned through the pain. Her aunt and uncle paced back and forth with her. They were like two crutches under her arms. "My back is hurting so bad, can I just lie down?"

"No, you heard Piti. We have to walk with you until she comes back." The smart answer Moiselle had thought of was quickly swallowed when some invisible monster grabbed across her stomach. A few hours later, Piti rushed in. "Put her right there on the bed, let me she if she's opened up enough for the baby." Aunt Neila and Papa Boss supported Moiselle as she stumbled toward the bed. "Oh, that's better. You're opening. She's about to open." Piti put her thumbs and index fingers together to show how dilated Moiselle was.

All night it was her aunt who assisted the midwife, cleaned the baby and gave it to Moiselle. Moiselle cried because her baby was the most beautiful thing she had ever seen. She had the same newborn paleness as Charlotte, but there were no brown circles around her cuticles. This was a sign that Grace would probably keep her pale complexion. Moiselle didn't want to think about what that would mean. She was filled only with joy that she had crossed the river and not drowned. She ran her finger softly through the tufts of soft brown hair. Her rosy lips puckered and once in a while she stuck the prettiest tongue out. When the baby finally opened her eyes, Moiselle was sure that God had placed two small oceans inside her eyes.

"What are you going to name her?" Aunt Neila asked softly.

"Lagrace Donner Moises."

Moiselle paused to see if her aunt was going to marvel that she had given her baby her own last name, but her aunt didn't pry. If she had asked, Moiselle would have said she named her Lagrace because that was the only phrase she remembered Robert's father preaching in thick Kreyol. He said the word over and over during that revival: "La grace!" The word had been electrifying, sending the crowd into a shouting frenzy of "Praise Jesus!" every time. Instead, Moiselle offered, "Her name is Lagrace because I pray for God's grace."

Aunt Neila shook her head with a great big smile. Moiselle wondered if the pride her aunt had just shown in her choice of name was a sign that she should stop punishing herself.

Moiselle believed God had finally forgiven her when, five months after Lagrace was born, Robert Donner's revival crusade came to Croix des Bouquet---the very town where she was still living with Aunt Neila and Papa Boss. That night she approached her aunt and uncle, who were sitting on the porch and retelling old stories. Moiselle listened and wondered if this taking apart memories and re-membering them was part of growing up. *Would she be like that in few years?* Would she pour every memory out, measure it into the beaker of time, and then pour it back in her bottle of memories? Would the stories she told her daughter about her father over time gain a glossy, buffed-out roundness?

"Moiselle, don't stand there with the baby, come sit here on this bench," her aunt said.

"Thanks. She likes the cool air." Moiselle looked at the sleeping Grace. Moiselle marveled at how much she looked like Robert. Sometimes she even smiled like him. How can someone look so much like someone else, but also like herself too? Moiselle wondered every time she looked at Grace.

"Don't you dare expose the baby to that air? Keep her fully covered."

Moiselle smiled, not wanting to challenge her aunt on what was best for her baby. Besides, she could tell that Papa Boss wanted to continue his story-telling. She sat quietly between the two adults, rocking the baby.

"There he was," Papa Boss was saying. "His leg torn up and suffering. He could barely talk. I looked for his dog tag—that's what the Americans called this metal necklace they wore. It said Private Jake Cosmos. He grabbed my hands and said 'Don't let the girl die alone. Don't let me die alone.' I looked around and saw no girl. Still, you have to be respectful to a dying man. I said, 'Jake, you're not going to die alone and I'm not going to kill you—not yet.' I laughed, wanting to make him at ease, you know, take his mind off of dying. I told Jake, 'Two men should fight in honor. It would be dishonorable for me to kill you now.' I cleaned his wounds and stopped the bleeding, but he was already turning white and his leg an even deeper shade of green than his uniform. 'The girl is about two miles. An animal with two legs attacked her. I was getting her help. Lucky for him I still had some soursop leaves in my satchel. I made him a strong brew and that helped him sleep off the pain.

"We slept. When I woke up I saw that sometime in the middle of the night he had crawled near the small fire to hold my hand. His hands were cold and stiff. I didn't have the proper tools, but I buried him, put a placard above the mound and I wrote all I knew. And this here is his bible." He held out the burgundy colored Bible with tattered edges.

"I thought you sent it back with his other things when you met that American news man five years ago. Remember, the one who put your story in the newspaper?" Aunt Neila said.

Papa Boss pursed his lips, waiting for his turn to talk, "I sent most things, but I wanted something to remember Jake by. I was thinking we could use this book to go talk to the young man who made this beautiful baby with Moiselle. I heard he is back in town."

Moiselle's eyes widened in alarm. *Of course they would know. Everybody knows everything around here.* It was a bit of a relief that they knew and wanted to get involved, but somehow Moiselle felt she should handle things herself. Besides, she asked herself, how is the Bible of a dead man going to help patch things between her and Robert? She didn't dare ask.

Moiselle sat next to her aunt, knowing what she wanted, but pacing her questions. "Aunt Neila, did you hear about the accident in the big market today?"

"I saw Marie-Maude and some of the neighbors talking and rushing towards town but I didn't know. What happened?"

"A bull got loose and impaled several people."

"You don't say!" Aunt Neila was shocked.

How much time will be enough if I find Robert and confront him so that it wouldn't seem that I was gone too long? "I want to walk over to Claudette's house to see if she is okay, and then I want to stop by the marketplace to see if my mother is there today, but I don't want to take the baby with me."

"Girl, you better not think of taking that sweet little baby. Go ahead, take a few of the avocadoes Papa Boss brought from the farm for Claudette. Hurry, because if she is hungry I'm going to breastfeed her and you know Charlotte doesn't like to share her mommy's milk."

Aunt Neila, lost in cooing at baby Grace, didn't see Moiselle go in the opposite direction of Claudette's house. Hurriedly, Moiselle pushed the brush away, kicked at a yelping dog, and dodged tree branches. She rehearsed several scenarios: *He will come to me and try to kiss me. I will slap his face nine times—one for every month he missed during my pregnancy. What kind of man are you? What kind of a man says he loves a girl and leaves? Do you remember by the river, how you made my body shiver?* Goosebumps ran along her arms. *Maybe I won't say it like that. I don't want him to think I want him to make love to me right there. I will kick him in the balls. That's for the white woman you chose over me. Did you think I wasn't going to know? Did you come back to have me as your concubine while your beautiful white woman stays as your wife? No, don't touch me.*

She stopped walking. *But what if he says he loves me and wants to marry me? Then, I will only slap him three times—maybe four.* When she resumed, her feet seemed to be going at a pace that could rival any thoroughbred. The scenarios flapped in her head like birds circling. She was so preoccupied that she nearly walked past the church grounds. Had it not been for the rise in "Hallelujah," she would have continued on to the end of the world.

Sure enough Robert was preaching, holding the Bible over people's heads. He wore his crisp white shirt, black tie, and black pants. Moiselle took in a breath and felt something drop into the bottom of her stomach. Since she was the only one not shouting and sweating and gyrating to the music, she was very noticeable. Robert's eyes found and held hers. His look pained her, his longing called to her. She rolled her eyes away.

Several things he said she felt were to get her attention: "Forgiveness is the reason, brothers and sister, Jesus came. You and I are not worthy. I'm a sinner and a coward." He repeated those words and still she didn't look at him. He walked to the back row where she stood. "Are you a believer, sister?" he asked Moiselle, rubbing the Bible on her head. She remained stiff. "Let's say a prayer to bind this spirit of willfulness in this woman, church," he said, and everyone, with closed eyes, began to pray out loud. He leaned close to Moiselle as if praying over her head, and whispered, "Meet me by the cemetery." Then, the crowd's praying dwindled. He moved back to the front and resumed his preaching.

After a few minutes, she held his eyes. She wanted to make sure he chased her. Just as his voice came down from a feverish pitch, she exited the tent. She stood out there, counted to ten, and heard him call on the band to play music so that he would be free to come outside the tent. When she heard the flap she turned, looked at him, and ran.

Did he think we would walk together to the cemetery?

"Moiselle!" he called in a husky whisper.

She ran towards the cemetery. He tried to catch her, but with the wind running through her hair, she felt that old freedom—like she wasn't someone's mother, someone's meal. Like she was Moiselle again and Robert hadn't left her.

As he reached for the tail of her skirt, she accelerated. He grunted and she disappeared through the woods. When she got to the mermaid tomb, she stopped and watched him trudge in. He was out of breath. He tried to stabilize his breathing. Watching him holding his knees, trying to catch his breath, erased all of the rehearsed words and scenarios.

"Fifteen months, Robert? What happened to your promise to return? I thought a week or month at best."

"Sh. . ." he said standing up, placing his hands on her shoulders, and then putting his index fingers over her lips.

She jerked away from his touch.

"All by myself I had your baby, coward!"

"Baby?" He leaned against the peeling stucco of the cemetery's gate post. "I don't believe it, Moiselle. I never spilled inside of you."

"A girl, if you care. I'm staying at my aunt and uncle's house on Rue Stenio Vincent, if you want to see us. I won't meet with you like this again."

The next day, Moiselle moved things around the house and forgot to put them back where they should go. She stared out of the window every fifteen minutes, wondering if Robert would come. Phillip and Victor were home from school. She tried to catch one or two words from their speech—fast as a windmill.

"And there must be twenty white people at the school. Father Moran made us sing for them yesterday. And he said they will build a real school with walls for us. That way when it rains we don't have to go home."

"That's not all he said, Phillippe. Don't you remember he said we would have new pews?"

Moiselle smiled at them but her every thought was on Robert. Finally, when she couldn't take their chatter anymore, she said, "Go fetch some water for me and tomorrow when I make coconut patties, I will give you an extra one."

She hadn't finished talking when the boys were already flying out of the door, heading in the direction of the river. She heard them giggle and say, "Good morning, Mr. Blan, Mr. White man."

She ran to the window and saw a fresh-shaven Robert approaching. She ducked from the window.

Robert knocked on the door and Aunt Neila opened it. Moiselle couldn't believe that Grace woke up at that precise time and gave a small cry; Moiselle could not hear Robert's first words to Aunt

Neila, but her aunt was speaking unusually loudly: "Oh, yes. I am her aunt and my husband is resting. Let me get my husband for you." Moiselle wondered what her aunt thought of Robert. When her aunt came to the room, she said, "You won't believe who just arrived!" Moiselle feigned ignorance and her aunt continued, "Your Robert is here. Papa Boss is speaking with him in the living room. What do you think?"

"I have no idea. I hope Papa Boss puts him in his place."

"Well, I know you're angry, but he seems like such a nice guy. He is so handsome and those eyes are just like Lagrace's." Moiselle pretended like she wasn't excited, but inside fireworks were exploding. She wanted her aunt to leave the room so she could dance. "Let's dress the baby in that pretty pink matching bonnet and dress, and you should wear that new dress Marie-Maude gave you before you got pregnant."

Moiselle changed as her aunt took care of Lagrace. When she arrived in the living room, her aunt handed the baby to Robert. His face lit up when he saw her. Lagrace cooed at him and he laughed.

"She has such a great personality," Aunt Neila said.

He kissed her, saying, "Grace is a good name. By the Grace of God we are granted this precious baby." Robert, like everyone else before him who had seen the baby and thought Lagrace was too complicated a name, called her Grace. Moiselle wondered if Grace liked everyone truncating her name because as soon as everyone started to agree and repeat "Grace" she started to cry. Everyone laughed and Moiselle reached for her from Robert. Their foreheads touched and she could smell the lemongrass, anise, and mint lotion she had made for him to repel mosquitoes.

Papa Boss sat observing while Robert squirmed. He pulled his nine-month-old baby girl, Charlotte, onto his lap. As he stroked her cheek he said, "Robert, you see that Bible on the table, take a look."

Robert picked up the Bible on the small table, under the lantern. He opened it and a piece of paper fell out. He unfolded it and started to read the article. "This article is written by my father and it's about you." Robert's eyes widened.

"The world is very small. I realized the connection just a few days ago when I saw your crew setting up your revival tent. I asked around and they told me this was the traveling crusade of Pastor Colvin Donner and his son, Robert Donner. Moiselle had said your name once or twice and I just figured there couldn't be two people with the same name in this small area. So yesterday I told her that I was going to use that Bible as way to open conversations between our two families. It's like our spirits communicated and here you are today."

"Yes. My father wrote for the church organization's newsletter, which was sent back to America every year. I didn't even know there were copies distributed here. He will love this, do you mind if I show him?"

Papa Boss nodded. "As long as you return it. It's my only copy."

"My father is going to be so happy. He had some disputes with some people last time he was here, so he decided not to stay at the church grounds. He's staying at the sanatorium. The doctor in charge is a good friend. Do you think we could bring it to show him?"

"Well, Brother Donner, I was hoping for a reunion so we could talk about this business between you and Moiselle." The smile left Robert's face and worry rolls formed on his forehead. "Five years ago, when your people came here, I felt the spirit and I accepted your Jesus as my savior. What has happened here between you and Moiselle is not acceptable in Jesus' eyes."

Moiselle wanted to see what Robert would say. The two men sat with the previously spoken words like ropes around their hands. Robert said nothing. He kept his head bowed as he nodded in acquiescence, "I will talk to my father and set up a reunion. He might not want to come this far out from the revival, would you come to the church grounds?"

"This is my country and I have no problem walking any time of the day to go anywhere. Just say the word." Robert got up and stroked the sleeping baby's cheek, but his eyes were on Moiselle. She pretended to be wiping something off the back of Grace's leg. Finally Robert said, "Good night, sir. May I have your permission to have a word with Moiselle outside? We won't go past the gates."

Papa Boss acquiesced and Moiselle thought to put the baby down before going outside, but she didn't trust herself. The baby would be a good barrier between them, she reasoned.

Outside, the moon was stingy—only a sliver hung in the sky like a crumb of a once giant cookie. Grace on her shoulder, she leaned against the gate in front of the pink oleanders. He was silent, stroking Grace's soft curls. "You see this pout she does with her lips? My mother used to do that. When she first smiled at me, I swear it was like looking at my mother's face." Moiselle pretended she didn't hear those words. She knew how much his mother meant to him, and a year before she would have walked to the moon to give him something that would make him remember his mother in a loving way, to replace that last image he had of her in the river. A year ago she would have wanted to replace the dying face of a drowning woman, hung on a rope, with the angelic face of a baby for him, but now her anger was like a big stone covering the soft earthiness of her heart. A long while passed and only silence flourished between them. "Do you have something to say or are you just going to look at me with that dumb look on your face? I have a baby to take care of, so I don't have time to just stand out here and stare at each other."

He inched closer. "I missed you." She looked at him, unblinkingly. "Your uncle is proposing that we make this official, what do you think?"

"How can you marry me when you're already married to *Lily White*? That's her name isn't it?" He placed his palm over his mouth, as if he was holding his panic inside. "You didn't think I would know. How could you, Robert?"

He dropped to his knees. "I want nothing but to always be with you, but I have a duty to my father--"

"Your father, what about *your child*?"

"That's just it. I didn't know about her, so now that I know, I'm willing to do what's right. I will call off my engagement with Lily and, if you'll have me, I would like to be your official husband."

Moiselle looked in his eyes and they seemed to be true, but she told herself that she had seen that true look before. The soft purring of the sleeping baby against her neck reminded her that she wasn't making a decision for herself, but also for Grace. She didn't want to look in his eyes. She didn't want him to think her answer was easy. She started to walk away. Half way between the gate and the porch, she turned and said, "Yes, I'll have you."

Colvin sat in Doc's dimly lit office. Their shadows cast against the textured walls, showed them as stooping men. Colvin uncurled his spine so that his shadow would straighten up, too. The room was built without a window—a fortress, he thought. "So, basically, if the loonies ever turn on you, you can come and hide in here," Colvin snickered.

Doc leaned back, and the chair creaked under the weight of his belly, a spherical wonder. "It's more likely that the outside world will attack me before my patients would." He removed his glasses from his wide nose and wiped them with the edge of his floral printed shirt. Colvin's eyes lingered on the orange walls and the primitive pictures painted there. Most were of faces with crosses and a few had open mouths with what looked like truncated tongues. He wondered if Doc held sessions in this room with his patients. He was relieved when Doc said, "Several of my patients can't talk. During the occupation, they cut off their own tongues when the Americans captured them rather than talk. It was a break-through for them to paint their stories on that wall. I'm still trying to piece it all together."

"And you're supposed to be the sane one?" Colvin mocked.

"I'm surprised you came here and asked to stay for a few days. The last time I saw you, you called me a devil worshipper, a nigger-lover, and stormed out of here. That was almost five years ago."

Colvin's face and neck were red. He chuckled, "Well, maybe you should check me in. Analyze my head and stuff. I mean, was I wrong? You go to voodoo ceremonies and you take one of those voodoo worshipers to bed every night." He paused and cracked his knuckles, as if he was getting ready for some street fight.

"I hope you've changed your ways, Colvin." Doc leaned forward to grab a button that had come off his shirt.

Colvin squirmed in his seat. He thought this was a good place in the conversation to change the subject. "This place hasn't changed one bit. I remember when I first returned to Haiti in `34, you picking me up from Port au Prince all excited about finally doing the work that the Navy hadn't let you do during the occupation."

Doc mumbled and grunted, a sign Colvin took as acknowledgment. Doc wrapped his plump fingers around the black handle of a small, pewter bell. He shook it vigorously. A minute later, a young man in an oversized shirt, wide grin, and aloof eyes appeared. Doc said, "Bosquin, please bring us some lemonade and anything that is still good to eat."

"Yes, sir," Bosquin affirmed, disappearing as fast as he had come. Then, Doc sat at the edge of his chair and leaned in closer to Colvin, as if he was about to reveal a secret.

"Trust me. There's been changes. Come here." He lifted a quilt that was hanging against the wall. A brown door appeared. Doc opened this door and pointed upward. "You see here. We now have to have guards with guns at the top of the asylum to protect us down below." Doc quickly closed the door when he heard Bosquin coming. Bosquin placed the tray of drinks and sweet potato bread on the table. Doc patted him on the back as he crossed in front of him. Once Bosquin closed the door, Doc whispered, "A few months ago we were attacked. There is a rumor that most of the prisoners here are being held under pretense. That the women are former Cacos guerrillas called Cocottes."

"Well, there goes my theory that I could come stay in a safe place while my son preached in Croix des Bouquets," Colvin said, sipping his lemonade to hide his apprehension.

<u>Two nights after Moiselle accepted Robert's marriage proposal, Aunt Neila and Papa Boss accompanied Moiselle and baby Grace to the revival as arranged by Robert. Robert's speech was quiet—like a defeated general. "Our days intertwine like the braided fibers of a rope. Each encounter or decision crosses another, therefore braiding a complicated life. Life ties us up, hangs us up, yet, we can use it to tie ourselves to an anchor," he said as he stared at Moiselle. The audience stood up clapping and shouting. He motioned for them to sit so he could continue. Then, he reached his hands out to the audience, as if unleashing invisible powers from within, and yelled, "Brothers and sisters, repent!" With tears streaming down his face he said, "I am not worthy. I have done wrong. I would like to repent and ask my God for forgiveness."</u>

Moiselle squirmed on the bench as the silence seeped in like rising floodwater. She was grateful for the baby, to uncover, cover, and burp—even when the baby didn't need it.

After what seemed like half an hour of praying silently while the audience watched, Robert stood up. "Church family, I want to introduce you to my own family," he said, beckoning for Moiselle to join him up on the make-shift stage.

The crowd cheered. Wings that Moiselle didn't know she had carried her to his extended arms. Robert scooped up the baby and presented her to the crowd and the music started. Moiselle smiled as she scanned the crowd. Most of these people she had seen in passing or knew. There were relatives of a relative, there were people she knew from years of going to the market with her mother, and there were neighbors of her parents. She was sure they had written her off as a whore. Her story was going to be so different now that he had claimed her.

But the crowd's dancing around made her stomach tighten. It meant her story was changing. Their movements were like a hammer pummeling her into the soil, planting her deeper. All of her dreams to leave this place seemed at the tip of her fingers with his public acknowledgement, but slipping away with the crowd's elation. *They will need me to stay here and be a testimony to my new story—the girl who made the white man weep or the girl who, despite challenges, snagged a handsome white American.* The thought that she now had a duty to stay nauseated her. She was going to have to stay so that when they wanted to prove and point to *that* girl they could find her: walk by her house, point to her grave, and point even to a star in heaven. Moiselle's feet felt like they were stuck in mud; they didn't move with the rhythm.

As the last of the crowd returned to their seats, her eyes fell on four people standing at the back of the tent. Someone must have gone home to retrieve them. Her mother had a blank look as she held her brother and her sister by the hand. She knew her father wouldn't cross the threshold based on his accusation that "White people have captured God and made him small enough to put in their pockets."

From where Moiselle stood on the make-shift stage next to her crying, just-become husband, her father's eyes bore into her, calling her traitor. They pulled words embedded deep in her memory. Words that she may have heard in the crib: *How could you? Her father thought. The Americans hate us. They treat us like we are not humans.* She shuddered at what he would say had he known that Robert's father was instrumental in the capturing of his hero. Her father turned to leave. Her mother stood for a minute longer, waving. It was the kind of wave that spread an ocean between two people. Moiselle held her hand up in response and the crowd cheered, interpreting it as a sign of praise to God.

After the revival attendants had gone, Pastor Denis married the two lovers. It was a simple ceremony of repeating words that Moiselle didn't understand. How can someone know what better or worse is? How can someone promise what will happen tomorrow? But wasn't this what she wanted? She said the words, and the soft thud of the minister placing the Bible on their heads and praying shook the questions away.

Moiselle looked around and saw that only her aunt and uncle remained. There was no one to represent Robert. *He has done this against his father's will. He chose us.* She didn't realize she had a serious look on her face until Aunt Neila said, "I thought getting married was going to make you happier." As they exited the tent, Moiselle whispered loud enough for Robert to hear, "I will be happy when he brings back the marriage certificate from Port-au-Prince to make it official." Her aunt's eyebrows furrowed and then Moiselle added, "I hope he doesn't think I'm just going to accept a church wedding."

Robert gave her what she called, "his uneasy smile" and said, "I'm going through the back to get a few things. In the morning, I'll come to get the rest."

He walked towards the front door where his father and step mother usually stayed. Moiselle saw Robert reach that doorstep in less than twenty strides. She moved close enough to hear, but hid behind a tree. Robert said, "Beverly, I'm not sleeping here tonight. If my father should return from the asylum or should he send a message for me, tell him to get directions to where I am from Pastor Denis." His stepmother didn't open the door. Moiselle wondered if Lily White was in there. She imagined walking up to Lily White and saying, "Yes, I'm Mrs. Robert Donner. How do you do?"

Poupette Moises didn't return home with her husband after witnessing Moiselle's church-tent wedding. She waited in the shadow of the revival tent, knowing Eveline Denis had seen her when she flashed the red flag. They walked together hand and hand, as they had as children. When they got to the river, Poupette said, "You're always saying that Cocotte is a beast with no head and no tail."

"Of course, I have been managing things, but we don't have leaders," Eveline Denis responded.

"That's good to hear. So, you'll understand that we didn't go behind your back, Eveline."

"I'm glad you feel like that. I didn't know the wedding was going to happen. Papa Boss showed up with them and my husband doesn't know that Robert is the animal's son and that's why he married them."

Poupette was silent for a minute. "That's not what I was referring to when I said we didn't go behind your back. I'm talking Cocotte business. The sisters are angry that the animal has returned to Croix des Bouquets after what he did to your maid and then sneaking away in the middle of the night to escape her brother's machetes. I wanted to get you away in case things got violent."

"Violent? Poupette, at some point you're going to have to talk about this. Your daughter may have married her own brother or at the very least, your rapist's son!"

"Wait a minute--what changed? Last time we talked you encouraged me to remember the possibility that she was Champagne's child and not the animal's." Poupette walked away for a minute. Then, she turned back to face Eveline, "You know there are times I can still smell that animal's rancid smell. Like vomit in my mouth choking me, moving inside of me. His beard rubbing against my fucking neck! No, I don't want to talk. I want his blood."

Eveline rushed to her and hugged her shoulders. "I'm sorry, Poupette. Even if they are related, it happens all the time. All over the world I'm sure."

Poupette leaned her chin against Eveline's head, "It's better not to wake the sleeping dog," Poupette said, so quietly as if trying to convince herself.

Suddenly, Eveline gasped, like remembering an item left on a stove. "Did you say that Cocottes are on my property? What about my children and husband? What if they get hurt? We never bring harm and attention to ourselves. The animal is not even staying on my property."

"What are you talking about? We were told that he always stays in the little cottage in the back--"

"No, He's been staying at the asylum, visiting his friend Doc." She stressed the last word, then held both of Poupette's hands and pleaded, "Call off whatever is planned for tonight. We need to meet at the Houmfort tonight for a new plan."

"Okay. I'm going to try to find the women deployed and spread the word. What time at the Houmfort?"

"Midnight--to plan something for tomorrow!" Eveline yelled back over her shoulder.

The women parted ways, each going in a different direction.

Eveline ran the half mile. Fat, billowing smoke rose against the dark night's sky from her guest cottage. She couldn't see the blaze, so before going to the cottage where she knew Beverly Donner and Lily White to be sleeping, she rushed to wake her husband and children. "Daniel, di fe. Fire! Wake the boys up and get them out." She banged on the door of her three-room cottage. Six women who helped her around the church in return for food, often found shelter in the church building, which was the farthest from the fire. The women came out and instinctively scrambled to get buckets of water from the nearby well.

Daniel Denis staggered outside their cottage bare-chested and bare-footed, in his shorts. His love-handles jiggled as he skipped from foot to foot, complaining about the biting pebbles. The boys, like all children who have built-in sensors for danger, rushed to the back of the guest cottage. The look on their mother's face reigned in their excitement and they ran back toward the church building to gather other children to come watch. Most of the water the church women brought fell on the brown soil on the path from the well. So, when they threw it on the back of the cottage where the blaze raged, it didn't make any impact. Items inside the walls of the cottage sizzled and popped as they melted. Panic seized Eveline, who knew not to touch the door's metallic handle. She said to her husband, "Daniel, we need machetes to hack the door down and get those two women out of there."

"I can't run fast enough without my shoes. Why don't you run to our cottage. Right behind the side door, I have a machete and a pickaxe. In the meantime, I'm going to try different things," Daniel Denis explained.

Eveline ran back to her cottage while Daniel brought the force of his weight upon the door. It creaked, but didn't budge. "Beverly?" he yelled as he banged on the door. "Don't stand behind the door." Finally, a faint, "Okay" came from Beverly's side of the door just as Eveline arrived with the machete and a pickaxe. Daniel took them without a word and began to whack the door in the middle with the sharp ax. Wood pieces flew in every direction while the sound of dry palm fronds used for roofing crackled like the laughter of old delirious women. After a few whacks, sweat poured down Daniel's body. He finally made a hole big enough to kick the door with his foot. Both he and Eveline ran into the cottage. Lily White and Beverly sat huddled inches away from the flames.

The next day Pastor Daniel Denis sent word to Robert that Beverly and Ms. Lily White had left. The messenger boy, proud to be given such an important job, recounted what he had heard. "Pastor said devils come to attack and take the white women."

"Hush, boy." Moiselle said, not wanting Robert to hear. She feared if Robert heard that news, he would try to go with the women to protect them. Where would she be now that they had reconciled? She said nothing as she took a bag containing a burgundy colored Bible and a rope from the boy. Moiselle recognized the rope right away. It was the rope Robert had been carrying when they first met at the well. Was this the rope Champagne had cursed? She wondered and made a note to ask Robert.

After the wedding ceremony, they returned to the home of Aunt Neila and Papa Boss. Victor and Phillippe were moved out of the room they shared with Moiselle to give the newlywed privacy.

"I know they gave us the room, but we can't stay here for long. When I go back on the road, I don't want anyone to monitor my goings and comings," he said as he got ready for bed. She stayed silent.

"Did I do something wrong?" he asked, and then corrected himself, "Other than to be a coward and leaving you while you were pregnant?" She shook her head as a welcomed yawn escaped her mouth. He had stripped to his underwear and lie on the medium sized bed. "Are we going to talk and make-up or do you want to be mad at me forever?"

She ignored him. "You make all the decisions. You want us to stay here. Live and die here. Why didn't you keep us with your family at the church?"

"Moiselle, you just love to pick a fight, don't you?" He turned onto his stomach. She kept waking up the baby and pretending to feed it until Robert fell asleep. She placed the baby in the wicker basket that her aunt used to take to market, but with some decorating had made a crib for Grace. A few minutes later, Robert was in an open-mouth snore when she grabbed a cloth wrapper that the women used when bathing by the river. She tiptoed past her aunt and uncle's bedroom and watched her little cousins sprawled on their mats on the living room floor.

She wanted Robert's arms around her, but she was still too mad at him to let it happen. She admitted that she was more annoyed than mad. She thought after the wedding they would leave Croix des Bouquets and travel, but he made the decision to keep them there. She had heard that newlyweds went on honeymoons for at least a few days. He made no mention of that. They could leave the baby with her aunt and go. Wasn't she special enough?

Moiselle followed the half-moon toward the river. The incessant drum sound she called night music, which played most nights, echoed in the distance. She wished there was more light, but she knew the path—every dip in the gravel road, every tree around the bend, and the spots with scurrying animals. Twenty steps this way the mango trees and two steps this way the gravel path became muddy. She knew where to reach into the ylang-ylang tree to snap several yellow flowers. She bent lower and gathered acacias, then reached for a few Lady of the Nights and red hibiscus along the way. She sat by the river's edge, at the very spot where they had met and made love so long ago, and adorned her hair with the white flowers. She didn't notice that Robert had been following her. An anger began to grow in Robert: was she meeting someone here—the very night of their wedding? He waited to see if someone came. She disrobed and entered the water and began scrubbing herself with the flowers and leaves she had picked along the way. He closed his eyes as the heavenly scent he had known as Moiselle came to him.

Robert approached her and was surprised at how quickly Moiselle scrambled to the bank to grab a knife. Where had she stored it? "Oh, it's you," she said, rolling her eyes.

"Expecting someone else… to fight and dig that knife into?" She gave a nervous laugh and placed the knife back under her clothes. "I know what it looks like. Like I was following you because maybe I don't trust you, but it's not that," he said.

She turned her back and continued to wash her body with her aromatic floral arrangement. The moon beamed over her body and he nearly doubled over with desire. He remembered how good she felt in his arms and how much he had thought of her while he was gone. Some nights he ran for hours to forget the tight comfort of her body. There were days he didn't leave his bed because longing for her hurt so much. He approached her and when he was a breath away, he encircled her with his arms. She took in a breath and shuddered. She didn't fight him as he thought she might. But she didn't reach for his face as she had done in the past.

"Where did you go? Where were you these fifteen months? Did you have sex with that woman?"

"I...I was saving souls. Preaching."

"Saving Lily White souls."

His arms dropped. He felt dizzy. His gaze narrowed, *how do you talk to one woman about another one?* He decided it was not wise to ever talk about Lily to Moiselle. He was sure men talking to their women about other women was how wars were started. He pulled her in again. She shoved him and he fell back in the water. He thrashed until he gained his footing and then pulled her in with him. His face ended up on her breast and he nibbled. He held on to her nipple, which made her moan and shriek. When he lifted her out of the water onto the river's bank, she wasn't fighting him anymore. They ravaged each other's bodies the way one tears into a meal after days of starvation. Night jasmine and ylang-ylang fluttered around them, wrapping them in a cocoon, and their moans became the perfect melody for the accompaniment of a cricket concerto.

Robert sunk most of the generous sum he had amassed during his ten years of traveling and preaching into a small piece of land bought from Papa Boss. Within three weeks he had built a one-room house. At the entrance of the house, he hung a sign he had made one night thinking of his father's hasty departure. The sign said: "God bless this union."

As he carried Moiselle over the threshold, he said, "This is for now. When we have more kids, I'll add to this house and make it bigger."

Moiselle didn't understand why he insisted on carrying her inside the house. He explained that in America it is a tradition for a husband to carry his new bride into their new home for the first time. Moiselle loved that idea. "You'll carry me like that again when you take me to America and buy me a house there?" she asked. He laughed, panting, as if her flimsy weight had tired him out.

Moments later, Grace, who had been napping in the new crib that her father had made, woke up from her parents' laughter. Moiselle scooped her up. They went to the newly planted garden. Moiselle noted that already there were weeds in the garden. She gave the baby to Robert and began to pull weeds between the eggplants, tomatoes, and peppers. Despite Moiselle's protest, Robert placed Grace on the moist, brown soil. She was crawling on her belly. Moiselle stopped weeding to watch her fat, dimpled thighs, her dark honey hue, her soft curly afro, and her perfect plum lips. Moiselle began to cry.

"What's wrong?" Robert asked, as he dropped the tools he was cleaning and began to rub her shoulders. The sobs were short and brought to mind a wounded animal. Robert just held Moiselle.

"I can't believe I thought about getting rid of her." The sobs started again.

Robert gently lifted her chin so that his green eyes shed light on her face. "You were lonely and going through something very emotional. You have to forgive yourself."

She accepted his explanation, as he held their daughter and whispered a lullaby to them both in English. Moiselle didn't understand the words, but she liked how crisp English sounded, like cutting and digging into iceberg lettuce. English words didn't linger; they had a job to do and they knew it. She couldn't wait to go to America and learn them. She decided not to bring up the topic again, for last time it brought on a small argument. For now she just allowed herself to be rocked in the arms of her husband as they held their baby.

Later that night, as they lay contented in bed after a night of slow love-making, she sat up and said, "Robert, it's been almost three months, when are you going to get our marriage certificate from Port-au-Prince?"

He paused and sighed. "I can't tear myself away from those purple lips," he said, laying kisses on her nose.

"I'm serious. I'm not stupid. We're not really married without that piece of paper."

"Who told you that? Of course we're married. The only marriage that counts is in the eyes of God."

She turned away from him. He stroked her shoulders, but she didn't turn. He kneeled on the bed and put his chin to her shoulder said, "You want to know how much I love you? I'm gonna tell you a very big secret." That got her attention. She turned to face him with a raised eyebrow. "The secret is—and this is between us," he whispered. "You know how I told you I have to go to Port-au-Prince to get Bibles? Well, the real reason is that some of the Bibles have money in them." He reached for a box under their bed and showed her the decoy Bible.

She placed her hand over her mouth. "I have seen this Bible a million times and never thought that it had money in it, you sneak!"

"Well, that's how our American congregation sends money to us. This way it doesn't get stolen. Who reads or look through Bibles?"

"That's smart," she said, marveling at the Bible.

"Next time I go to Port-au-Prince, I'll go make the marriage certificate. But I can never get out of here. Just last week I said, I'm going to go to Port-au-Prince and even hit the road to preach for a week or so, but as soon as I make up my mind, you seduce me."

"Oh, you're gonna know seducing when I'm done with you to-night," she said, pushing him back on the bed.

He murmured, "You're my anchor," his voice full of rapture.

She smiled and thought back to the night they got married in the church. *He had said that word*, but she decided she would ask him about that later.

Eveline plopped a red Bible on the floor in front of the Cocottes, who sat in circles. The shortest women were in the first row of the circle. The person who had the floor was in the middle. Eveline knew that their gasps were melodramatic—to encourage her. She circled the book a few times and then Surette, a young thin-faced woman, said, "I hope you don't plan on converting us all tonight, Mrs. Pastor."

Laughter came from the non-Christians who always sat on the left side, nearest the door, closest to the drum beats.

"Not even Jesus can help you, ladies," someone said. Eveline knew it had to be one of the handful of the women who had converted and attended her church. Eveline circled the book one last time. Its singed, frayed edges didn't obliterate the beauty of the gilded, unburnt spine. She opened it and stacks of green dollars spilled out. The gasps and laughter this time were real.

"Sisters, this is what that animal Colvin Donner kept coming back for. Now that the cottage is burnt and most of these Bibles too, I don't think he is going to come back. I don't know how many of these Bibles existed, but this is the only one that survived."

"If he's not coming back, that's not good news. That means he got away." Poupette stood, arms akimbo, shoulders hunched forward.

"Well, I have two things to talk to you about that relates to this money and the animal. First, we're going to use this money to feed girls. Half of it, $10,000 gourdes, will go to orphans. We'll vote on how to do that. The other half we're going to take to Port-au-Prince. It has to end up in the hands of specific senators, deputies, and politicians who will put our demands for mandatory national female education on the floor."

"Not to cut you off, Eveline, but that is not a lot of money. We should invest some of it so that the girls can eat not for one month, but for many years. We can pay the politicians a little bit at a time, not in one lump sum," Piti, the midwife said.

Uproar exploded out of the women. Eveline was grateful for the consistent drum beat in the background that masked outbursts like that.

"We have no head or tail, ladies. Talk Piti."

"Some of you won't remember, but when the Americans were here, we had to beat water to make butter. So when we had money, we would invest it. With this kind of money, we could buy five harvests of coffee, yucca, and or even breadfruit. Sell them and make five times the money."

The younger women clapped and the older women nodded, perhaps looking back into the past and simultaneously looking into the future. Several women stood up and discussed various healthy crops that could be purchased. Others stood to ask how they would keep the accounting. To this question the oldest woman stood, shaking and leaning on her cane, "We have never had distrust. Live or die Cocotte. If you steal from your mother, your sister, or your cousins, you die."

The women were quiet, perhaps remembering the few who had to be made examples of. Then, Eveline broke the silence, "Okay, all in favor of investing the money in this harvest, raise your hand. Only one hand, Surette." Everyone laughed, but all hands went up.

"Now, the second thing I want to talk about is going to give our veteran sisters relief. We are not going to let Colvin Donner get away. Does anybody have any thoughts on how we can do this?"

Neila Dubin held her sister, Poupette's hand and said, "I can keep an eye on his son."

Every hand in the room clapped, but Eveline interjected, "With three kids and a husband, you can't possibly keep an eye on him. I like what you're saying, though. The son will lead us to the father. Ladies, you know the saying, many hands make the load lighter. So, let's divide each day of the week. There are forty eight of us, so let's divide the days until our next meeting." The women talked and each woman had a specific day and hour of the day. For every hour there was a main woman and an alternate.

The women exited the tent led by Poupette, who suddenly was ensnared by the rapid fire of *nago* drum beats. Her scarred feet barely touched the ground as she twirled in the air, lifting her white skirt.

Robert threw himself into keeping a modest garden. They bartered with neighbors for what they didn't have. Neighbors and relatives marveled at the two working together in the garden. Moiselle giggled and smiled as if her face was going to rip whenever someone passed her and said, "Good morning, Madan Blan." This became her new moniker. She marveled at how many people knew her as Mrs. White Man.

On Sunday mornings, after breakfast, they would walk to church. Robert in the crisp white shirt, black tie, and black pants that Moiselle took pains in ironing. He carried Grace and Moiselle carried the red umbrella with the golden Chinese writings on it. Her mother had brought her the umbrella and only said: "A gift from a friend who could not be here." Moiselle had not pressed her because she knew who the friend was. As they walked to church under the glow of golden letters with pronouncement of good wishes, people came out of their houses to look, smile, wave, and sometimes they would say, "*Gade blan yo.*" Look at the white people.

Robert hated to be referred to as the blan, the white man. But as Moiselle told him, "When you live in a small town, you have no rights. You are part of the story and people christen you according to your most obvious characteristic."

"It's not right," Robert mumbled, not responding to anyone who called him Mr. White.

"Be thankful you didn't end up like my cousin who sells goats. He is known as George Goat."

Moiselle noticed that Robert was extra tense on Sundays. At first she wondered why they kept moving back two rows each Sunday. The first Sunday they went to Pastor Denis' church, they sat in the front pew. The next Sunday they sat in the third pew. That Sunday they sat in the very last pew of the ten-pew church, and Moiselle decided she had better ask what was going on.

"He hasn't even so much as asked me to read a verse. What kind of insult is that? I'm a much better preacher than he is," Robert said.

"I never realized it mattered to you to be part of his service."

"That's not the point. The point is he should acknowledge me." Moiselle started to say something and he stopped her. "I know that look on your face, Moiselle. Don't even think about saying anything to him or his wife."

"What?" she said innocently.

"Promise me."

She didn't say anything, she just went up to him and gave him a long, deep kiss.

On the last Sunday they would attend Pastor Denis' church, they sat in the third to last pew. After the singing and praise time, which was Moiselle's favorite time, Pastor Denis began to preach: "You know I like to be happy and show people that this is the day that the Lord has made, let us rejoice in it."

"Amen!" the congregation shouted. The older ladies with heads tied in their best silk *mouchwa* clapped and danced in circles. When the clapping died down, Pastor Denis continued to speak in that wide-toothed-smile way. "But, brothers and sisters, there is nothing that makes me sadder than the un-repented sinner." Moiselle perked up. She was so used to people whispering things about her, but she was relieved that all the eyes were not on her, but a young woman in yellow sitting two pews behind her. If Robert's arms were not around her shoulders she might have forgotten where she was and waved to the young woman. She caught herself before calling out to her, "Ingride". Pastor Denis bellowed from the pulpit, "In the Old Testament, the harlot's house was marked by the red painted window and that's how the men knew. But as we see here in Joshua, the harlot, Rahab, would be instrumental in saving the Israelites because she repented and believed." The congregation stood up and sang the key word, "Repent! Repent!" Moiselle was annoyed that she had to stand up every time the congregation stood to sing key words from the Pastor's sermon. Her hair was now plastered to her forehead. She stopped fanning Grace, who was passed out. She imagined that if they put Robert inside of a stove, he would not be any more red than he was. She said the loudest "Hallelujah" when Pastor Denis gave the benediction that ended the service.

Outside, a steady cool breeze began to restore their body temperatures. She handed the baby to Robert who carried her effortlessly. She saw in the distance that Ingride was walking behind them, going in the same direction. "Why do you keep looking back?" Robert asked. "Remember how when we first went by the river you asked me if I had friends?" He nodded, a smile crept across his face, "Get your mind out of the gutter. Well, you see that girl in the yellow dress behind us, she was in the back pew at church, and she used to be my friend."

"Used to?"

"We used to go everywhere together. The river, the market place. We just loved to chase each other until our bodies started changing and she started to make new friends. Soon, she was never around to go do the wash by the river. Then, about two years ago they sent her to Port-au-Prince when she got pregnant and the boy didn't speak for her. I had no idea she had returned."

"She's walking too fast. Her little daughter can't keep up."

"Robert, don't look back again. I think she knows we're talking about her and she is trying to get into her house before she gives us a chance to address her."

They turned left to go toward the main road and Moiselle looked back and saw the tail of Ingride's dress entering her cottage with the painted red window. Moiselle's mind flashed back to the day she saw Pastor Denis with the red paint and paint brush. She held on tighter to Robert's hands, shuddering at what would happen if she let go.

But Moiselle didn't stop being the topic of conversations in the town's market. People wondered about all that laughter coming out of the little blue cottage. "Sometimes, I feel watched," she said to Robert, who would look out the window and tease, "There's no one out there except for the ones watching us." They would laugh. Sometimes as she walked around selling the vegetables from their garden, she heard the whispers, "Oh, and one day, when I was walking by, it wasn't even one o'clock in the afternoon. The fire under the pot was turned off, the chicken in there marinating in its grease, and the window shutters shut. The sound, guuurl! coming from that little house made me run back home and grab my man to make some music too."

At times like that, when the tongues wouldn't stop wagging, Moiselle would ask, "Robert, when are we going to America? You told me you would take me to see great places." At times he humored her by breaking into American songs that she liked and dancing with her. Sometimes he told Bible stories, acting out the parts and making the voices. She loved when he made the lady voices. "When the king, her husband was going to kill her people, Esther saved them, she said, "Oh, my king. Please I have better use for your hands" he mimicked a woman. Moiselle laughed as he took her hands and placed them on his manly parts. She shoved him lovingly, and then he said, "The point of the whole story is in the story's fourth chapter, verse 14: everyone has a purpose," he said at the end of her favorite story. By then she had forgotten that she had asked him about going to America and spent her time imagining the life of Queen Esther. But when his patience was short because the days were too long, and he missed the curves and spontaneity of being on the road, he would instead give her a dose of reality. "In America they hang people like us. To them our marriage is an abomination. Remember my father's friend Benjamin? They would kill sweet baby Grace. Do you still think it is a great place?" Taking her silence and teary eyes as victory, he said, "God has given black people a piece of paradise right here."

The first time he said this to her, four or five months after their wedding, she left the house in tears. At first she didn't know where she was going. She headed towards Papa Boss's house, but turned the opposite direction. What were Aunt Neila and Papa Boss going to think? Less than six months of marriage and already fighting? Instead, she headed towards her father's farm. But she couldn't face her father. *If I go left, I'm going to end up at old Mr. Chin's. Moiselle, do you think that's a good idea? What if someone tells Robert? If I go and I feel the way I used to feel, does it mean I don't love Robert? What if I feel sad and miss Ling? Wouldn't it be something if Ling were there? Would he ask me about the jade ring? Okay, breathe. Mr. Chin is my friend. He is a family friend. Why shouldn't I visit him?* The last question lifted out of her head when Mr, Chin swung his door open and said, "Just in time for some tea, Zel."

It had been a while since someone called her by her childhood nickname. She didn't feel, as her nickname implied, like she had wings anymore.

"Zel, would you like to try some delicacies I brought back from my last trip to China?"

She smiled, shaking her head no. She stared fondly at the old man. Moiselle couldn't remember a time when he wasn't dressed in a three-piece suit. She wondered if he slept in his suits. She sat where he indicated. He always had records playing in languages that Moiselle didn't understand. Mr. Chin's cleaning woman, her cousin Marie-Maude, complained of him having a house so spotless that by the time she got there she didn't have anything to do. Marie-Maude also reported that many important officials came to visit Mr. Chin. When Moiselle's father called him a spy, Marie-Maude defended him. She told them he worked for the Chinese government and was sent to help Haiti. Despite the fact that Mr. Chin had helped him buy his property, it wasn't until recently that her father actually became openly amicable towards Mr. Chin.

"Your mother stopped by last week and she told me the good news. Congratulations, did you get my gift? How is the baby? Why didn't you bring her with you?" He placed his tea cup down.

Moiselle smiled, "Yes, I received the paper umbrella—it is beautiful and helpful. We use it when we're going to church or taking the baby anywhere. She's so fair, we don't want her to get heat rashes," she said, hoping that Mr. Chin would be impressed by the picture she painted of her family life. "She is also so heavy, and as Robert couldn't come, I didn't want to carry her all this way by myself."

She took advantage of the silence to explore the house with her eyes. What she liked about Mr. Chin's house was that it was like a foreign country. The things in his house made her imagine China. She saw people crowding around her to touch her skin, her hair, and in this vision, they loved her. On the ceiling of his modest house hung red paper lanterns and, depending on the time of day, they shone differently. In the windows, red flags with golden Chinese syllabaries glimmered. A golden dragon, which at first Moiselle thought was a snake, sat on the mahogany table, guarding.

Mr. Chin talked about the seasons coming and the furniture Moiselle's father had built and was going to build for him. His low murmur and the sound of soft music coming from the gramophone was relaxing. She thought about Robert, her baby, and their home. When she almost fell asleep, Moiselle stood and stared at the only picture on the cabinet in the living room. It was a younger Mr. Chin standing with another man. The other man was much taller than he was, but dressed in the same serious fashion. Both wore three-piece suits, but unlike the young man, Mr. Chin didn't have a striped red tie. His tall companion's smile lightened the somber portrait and he looked straight at Moiselle.

Mr. Chin sipped his coffee and said, "It was for the best Moiselle. I hope one day you can forgive Ling. You see how things worked out. You were meant to be with other people."

At this point, her eyes landed on the small jade stones in the picture frame. It jostled her memory back to the ring she had thrown down the well. Abruptly she said, "Sorry, Mr. Chin. I didn't want to leave for America without seeing you." She paused, wanting for her lie to sound believable. "I'm not sure where he's going to take me yet; his work takes him to so many interesting places. I just wanted to stop by. It could happen any day." She squeezed his bony arms as the tears stayed in her eyes under her strict command. She left in the same hurry she had come.

When she arrived home Moiselle found Robert in the garden and her heart sank because she saw he was getting too comfortable in Croix des Bouquets. "Did you have a good time visiting your mother?" he asked, assuming. Poupette often always visited on big market days so she could play with Grace, but she didn't sleep inside the house. "If your father asked, I don't want to lie and say I stayed at your house," she said. She always slept on the porch.

"Why don't you go back to preaching after the rainy season?" Moiselle said. "Can we travel together as a family?"

"Darling," he said, standing up, dropping a boniato he had dug from the soil. "The road is no place for my wife and baby girl."

"If you think I'm going to sit here and stew while you go around the world--"

"The road is long and uncomfortable. Trust me, it only looks appealing because you've never done it. It's no place for you."

"Do you miss it?"

"Yes, I miss preaching. I miss going into a new town and seeing new faces and wondering about the thoughts behind their sad or complacent smiles."

"Why don't you ask Pastor Denis to let you preach in his church?"

"Moiselle!" The exasperation in his voice was magnified by the thud of a hoe hitting the soil. "You think everything is so simple. How can I move in on his territory? People don't like that. That congregation is his flock. Beside, you act like I'm going to leave you and never come back. I will always come back—you're my anchor." He went into the small cottage and the door slammed behind him.

After the rainy season, Robert still hadn't left. He seemed to be content with expanding the garden. He even started to sell chickens and eggs. Sometimes, even though she was elated, her inner voice reminded her that he had also not gone to Port-au-Prince to retrieve the marriage certificate, but the thought of his going to get that document and then losing track of time and staying on the road for more than a night or two was worse than not having that piece of paper.

Often, she strapped Grace across her chest or on her back and went about her work. One bright day she had taken a basket of eggs and three chickens to the market, and she was so pleased because she had sold out before she had even made it to the market. She returned home early with so much excitement. From the top of the road she could see their little cottage with the blue shutters that everyone called the blue house, and she saw Robert on the porch looking in a Bible. The climbing vines and flowers surrounding the porch and his look of being lost in the Bible made her smile. When she got closer he was startled and he closed the Bible quickly. *Maybe he doesn't remember that he had told me about the Bibles.* She unwrapped Grace from her back and fanned her with a straw hat.

"Honey, I walked past the market to sell everything. I can't take one more step--will you please get me a drink of water?"

He tucked the Bible under his arm after he tucked some of his tools on the porch, and stood up. He kissed her forehead, cooed at Grace and went inside to get her the water.

Later, when Robert was asleep, she looked under the bed and found the Bible. She opened it, and there it was. Moiselle recognized the thin, elongated face and the cascading blonde ringlets of Lily White. She closed the Bible, tucked it back under the bed. She went outside for some air. She felt as if some had punched her in the stomach and there was no more air left in the world. She sat on the lower step of the porch. Soon Robert woke and joined her on the porch. A cool breeze caressed their skin. Does he regret our marriage? The thought gnawed at her heart. Many intimate moments flashed in her mind. How could he have said those things or touched her in those ways, yet still be thinking and looking at another woman's picture?

He didn't say anything. He went inside to retrieve Grace, whom Moiselle had placed on her mat for her afternoon nap, but Grace was wide awake. When he returned, they sat quietly watching Grace toddled after a lizard. He seemed simultaneously happy and sad.

"What's wrong, Robert?" she asked, hoping he was going to open up and confess.

"I'm going to have to go get the Bibles in a couple days. Pastor Denis stopped by and asked for my help. Apparently, his guest house burnt the day after my family left."

"Your family, Robert" she said and he saw the error in his speech. "You know what I mean. You and Grace are my family and so are they."

"Do you have to go right now?" she snapped.

"I've been putting it off for too long, Moiselle. I have to go tomorrow."

She stood outside the garden's gate. She didn't know what to say or think. "I don't want to deal with this right now. The garden is doing well--look." She dug in her pocket and retrieved the twenty dollars.

"The congregation is running low on cash and they need me to get the Bibles, and besides, I've put it off for almost a year now."

"Is this a song? You said that before," she nipped at him. It seemed so simple when he put it that way, but she kept thinking about the picture in his Bible. Tears filled her eyes, and she walked off with no specific plans in mind. She felt a little wind lift her off the ground and she felt the absence of Grace, but she didn't look back.

The sun was high and she didn't realize that her feet had taken her towards Beudet. She thought of visiting her parents, but she knew exactly where she wanted to go. She knew she wanted to be in a peaceful place where if there was judgment, it was never louder than the records playing. But the last time she was at Mr. Chin's several months before, she told him she was going to America. She would have to think of a convincing story to save face.

She grew thirsty and walked towards a bar that wasn't too far from her parent's farm. The wooden shack was painted yellow with the silhouette of dark figures in the throes of dancing-ecstasy. Broken shutters were leaning against a window. Wooden benches leaned against the wall. From the thatched roof hung whimsical charms made from plantain leaves. "Drunk and it's not even noon," Moiselle thought about a man with a hat covering his face. He was reclined with legs crossed, back against the wall. Moiselle grabbed a chair and the owner, whom she was acquainted with, approached with a plastic tumbler of lemonade—the drink of midday visitors.

"I'm just resting before I go back home. I didn't intend to come this far and I didn't bring money with me," she said, regretting having handed Robert all the money she had made that day.

"Don't worry about it; I'll pay for whatever she wants," came a voice from the shadow. Moiselle froze. It was like someone lit a match and stuck it at her feet. She knew that voice. Despite herself it echoed in her dreams, asking for his jade ring she had long tossed down her father's well the day she met Robert.

When a few hours passed, and Robert Donner's wife still hadn't returned, he put on a shirt, washed his face and took the baby with him to the only logical place she could be. Robert arrived at Papa Boss's house just as Papa was arriving from Beudet.

"Well, I'm happy to see you Robert, but to what do I owe this honor?"

Aunt Neila came out onto the balcony where Robert and Papa Boss had been sitting making small talk.

"Is Moiselle out back with you?"

"No, I haven't seen her since we went to market together two days ago."

"We had a little disagreement and she walked off. I thought she might have come to cool off here, but maybe she went to the market."

"Well, give me this luscious girl. Look at those cheeks. I just made something for Charlotte to eat, so Grace can eat too. I'll give her a bath, too."

Robert gave Aunt Neila a smile that showed he was grateful and relieved. He and Papa Boss spoke for another hour about the crop and farming. When Aunt Neila reappeared she asked, "Have you had supper yet?"

"No, Ma'am."

"Well, come on in. I just set the table for the boys, Papa, and me. We would love to have you."

After Robert said the prayer, they ate the mashed breadfruit dipped into the okra and herring sauce. Robert wished Moiselle were here to see it. She always made fun of Robert's inability to dip the mashed breadfruit and swallow it with ease. He didn't even chew this time. He swallowed like a native.

After dinner and coffee Robert decided to head home, but as it was drizzling Aunt Neila didn't want him to take Grace with him. He promised to return in the morning. He walked home and the little blue cottage was dark. Maybe she went to visit her mother? he thought. He walked towards Beudet—towards Moiselle's parent's farm.

He felt pangs in his stomach at the thought of having to sit under Mr. Moise's hateful glare. He liked Moiselle's mother very much. She came by their little house at least once a week, and there were always tearful goodbyes and feigned hurt when Moiselle wouldn't let her take Grace with her. Robert was surprised the first time he heard Moiselle's reason: "What if my father hits her?" and Mrs. Moise replied, "He's not mad anymore, let me take her please." Moiselle always said no.

Now Robert had to face that man. He admonished himself for getting into a silly fight with Moiselle earlier. *Why didn't I just humor her? I should have stuck to the plan and left while she was at the market. Why doesn't she believe that I will return?*

Halfway between his home and Moiselle's parent's home, there was a roadside home-turned-into-bar. Robert tried to read the name painted on the eaves of the thatched roof. He couldn't tell if it was "Lamou devaste" (love depleted) or "Lakou Desaste" (yard depleted). He chuckled at the irony in the missing letters. *What a difference one letter makes.*

He intended on stopping and grabbing just one shot of *tafia* to loosen him up so he could be ready for the old man's stares. Approaching the yellow shack, he saw two people slow-dancing. The man's face was buried in the woman's chest; his pale hands cradled her rounded butt. Moiselle liked places like this. He made a note to take her here when he returned from his trip.

Watching the couple, he wondered how he and Moiselle looked dancing slowly like that in the moonlight. The woman's shapely back reminded him of Moiselle. He looked away, feeling guilty that a woman who wasn't his wife turned him on.

"What do you have that's strong but will stay with me?" Robert asked.

The woman at the counter reached for one of six glasses she had on the counter. "I made this myself. Tell me if you taste the pineapple in it," she said as she filled his cup. The many bracelets on her arm jiggled and made music.

Robert thanked her and placed a Haitian half dollar on the counter. She smiled and continued to wipe chairs and greet customers. Robert turned his attention to the couple who danced that let's-have-sex-on-the-dancefloor dance no matter what song played. The music had gone from a slow bolero to the faster pace of the meringue, but they were still gyrating. When the bar owner changed the record, there was silence and the woman protested.

That voice cut through Robert like a big knife at a fist fight.

The inflection in her voice was like that of a baby whose rattle has been taken away. He realized why he had to squeeze his penis into submission as he had watched the dark figures dance on the floor. His body knew her every curve in that dress.

He ran towards the two and shoved them apart. The man stumbled back. His eyes were puffy slits, and in drunken, incoherent speech said, "Hold on there, fellow!"

Moiselle coughed up dust as she stumbled to the ground. "Ling, go home. You're only making things worse," Moiselle shouted at her dance companion. She wobbled as she tried to regain her footings to run after Robert. She grabbed at this shirt, but his shirt ripped instead.

"Get away from me, you slut." He shoved her back.

"Ling Chin is an old friend, Robert. We were just catching up on old times."

"Catching up? I hate to see what your reunions look like," he hissed. "I've had it with you, Moiselle!" Even in his anger, as he said the words, Robert was thankful that no one was around to witness their fight. His mind raced. As he tried to speak, he just saw images of her and the man. He imagined the man fucking her behind that bar. *Who knows--anything could have happened before I showed up.* He came closer to her face, pointing an index finger. "That wasn't talking you were doing. I'm done. No wife of mine is going to fuck around on me!"

Suddenly Moiselle's palms were wet. Her heart beat fast. She shook her head as if to get a terrible picture out of her head—maybe a picture of Robert's retreating back? Her bed without him? The garden without him? Life without him? The words were slower than the tears that dripped from her eyes, "I'm sorry. I am wrong. I shouldn't have done that." She dropped to her knees. "Forgive me, Robert. I will never do that again."

Robert squeezed his eyes shut. His mind went back to the first time they made love by the river bank and he was holding her, they were looking at the stars, and she told him he was the only one. That he didn't have to worry about anyone else. "Was this the guy that you told me I didn't have to worry about?"

She nodded her head up and down and said something in between hiccups and tears.

"I was such a fool! How could I not have asked more questions? How could I have not sought him out to investigate?"

"Well, you couldn't have. He was in China and just returned a few days ago."

His face contorted, as if tasting the foulest thing. "I gave up my father, my family, my faith for you, and this is how you repay me?"

"Robert." The word came out of her throat as if there was no space in there. "You made a choice. Just like I made a stupid choice today and I have to live with that. Don't blame me." She remained kneeled in front of him for several minutes longer. As she was getting up, she ran her hand over his thighs.

He didn't know why he was letting her approach him or why, despite himself, he stopped moving. Everything in him told him to run and not forgive, but the warmth of her hand felt so comforting. *Maybe she made a mistake. No one is perfect.* He thought about how things can lead to other things. How when he came in town, his plans were changed within a few hours of seeing her. Now, almost a year later, he still wasn't able to leave and do his work. A little voice chanted inside of him, *seventy times seventy*. He let her hug him. He didn't reciprocate. Somehow he knew he had to postpone leaving again. With this guy hanging around, he didn't trust Moiselle.

"I'll die if you leave me," she whispered as her lips closed over his.

The wind carried her words like it carried all the other light things floating in the air—away, away, to the sky.

The first time Robert left Croix des Bouquets was about a week after he found her at a bar, sex-dancing with her ex-boyfriend. When he told her his plans to resume the work of retrieving the Bibles, visiting different congregations to distribute Bibles, and do some preaching, Moiselle wailed like a child who was being pulled from its mother's breast. So he decided to take her with him. He reasoned that since they really didn't have a honeymoon when they got married two years before, he was going to make it happen.

The morning of their decision to go on this trip, Robert sold his hinny to a neighbor in exchange for some cash and the neighbor's young, male goat.

"This demands so much planning, are you sure you want to do this?" Moiselle asked. He had never seen her so happy.

"Yes, this is perfect timing because I want us to see Carnival. I want us to stay at a nice hotel. This is going to be the honeymoon we never had. I want you see the Champ de Mars. I want to take you dancing and one day, when we are old, we'll remember it as one of our best memories." Marie-Maude came from Beudet to watch and care for Grace, the house, the garden, and the livestock. She refused to take cash payment, but agreed to take two chickens.

Despite Moiselle's protest, Robert walked most of the way while she rode the mule they had bought from a neighbor. He wouldn't let her look in the bags he packed. She enjoyed it best when he sat behind her and she could lean on him and fall asleep.

In Croix des Bouquets people knew about their marriage, and very few people stared and pointed anymore. But that wasn't the case as soon as they left Croix des Bouquets. People stopped to look and point. "Keep your head up and don't look back at them," Robert said. "If you can't stand people looking at you five miles out of your town, then how do you think it would be for us to travel and be on the road?" She didn't say anything, but sat straight on the donkey, looking straight ahead, her straw hat providing shade from the rising sun. *This is the girl I fell in love with.*

They rode without stopping. When Robert was tired and the road was woodsy, he rode behind Moiselle, his arms around her. When they came to a paved road, they gave the donkey a break and Robert walked. The sun was already setting when they arrived at the Excelsis Deo Hotel. The wide expanse of the Champs de Mars stretched out like a big green bib in front of the hotel. The white wrought iron fence was like a tiara at the top of the hotel.

"Wait here. I'm going to find out where we can keep the mule." Robert disappeared between two green metal gates with scrolls that captured the dying sunlight. A few minutes later he returned. "This is Beauchamp, and he will take the mule, feed it, and take care of it. I have paid and have our room key." Robert dangled the key in front of her. They removed the two bags draped on either side of the saddle.

Climbing up the stairs, Moiselle marveled at the curved railings and limestone columns. Robert opened the door and her eyes went straight to the balcony, which overlooked the Champ de Mars. They stood on the balcony, Robert's arms around her watching the sunset. "If this is all you've planned, it is enough. I had no idea this much beauty existed," she said.

"Oh, I have so much more planned. We won't waste a minute," he teased.

While they stood watching the sunset, the maid had let herself in and brought the hot water Robert had requested and filled the tub. They lingered in the bath together. Robert splashed Moiselle with suds and she splashed him back. "Act your age. You're acting like a little boy," she teased.

"Can a little boy do this to you?" He touched her in the spot that always make her fold into pleasure. The intimate confines of the tub didn't limit their enjoyment of each other's bodies.

Later, she stood on the balcony taking in the view and he said, "I'm going to check up on the mule." Several minutes later, Moiselle's eyes caught sight of Robert talking to a woman. She wanted to see the woman's face. She told herself she had nothing to be jealous of, but still it bothered her.

A few hours later, Robert took her for ice cream and a walk around Champ de Mars. They walked to the cathedral. Looking up at the building, Moiselle asked, "Are all cathedrals pink?"

Robert hesitated, "I don't think so."

With a bounce in her step, she said, "Well, you're going to have to take me to every city with a cathedral so that I can find out."

Robert kissed her cheek and said, "You know what that round window reminds me of?" She shook her head. "The dial ring of a telephone."

"A what?" she asked and he laughed.

"Ok. They have one at the hotel. Look at that window and when we go back I'll show you the telephone. It's a device that allows you to talk to people who are in another city or country."

Her eyes grew three times their regular size.

"I want to see that. Let's go now."

He pulled her closer and said, "But we just got here. Let's listen to the music. It sounds so angelic."

She acquiesced, letting him lead her through the church's massive walnut-stained doors and ornate plaster work. They stayed for the mass. At the end Moiselle said, "I didn't think Protestants attended Catholic masses?"

He touched her nose, wiping the slight perspiration that had formed there. "It's an experience to sit here and take in the beauty of this cathedral. Look at the stained glass. Look at the architecture." After the mass, they walked silently back to the hotel, not caring about the long stares and the whispers as they passed people. One gawker even said, "I wonder if she's his prostitute?" to another. Robert stopped her, pulled her back, and kissed her deeply in front of those gawking French women. Then they laughed and rushed hand in hand toward the hotel. When she woke up from a nap, Robert wasn't in the room. She went down to the grounds of the hotel. In the distance, near the swimming pool, she saw Robert talking and laughing with one of the maids. She didn't like the way she looked up at him when she laughed. What was he saying to her? Why was he talking to her, she asked as she fumed away.

The next day Robert took Moiselle for a walk along the wharf because she spent the morning ignoring and giving him the silent treatment. He was amazed at the plaza that had developed. He took her to the fountain of the black nymphs. "I can't believe how much they've done in two years. The last time I was here they were only advertising it."

"This is so beautiful," she said, forgetting whatever was bothering her. She ran her hands over the bronze sculptures.

He took her to the site where he had witnessed a man giving his life for a little boy. "It happened right here. The little boy was concentrating so hard on flying his kite that he didn't see the car coming. The man jumped in and pushed the boy out the way. Just like that," he snapped his fingers, "He was dead."

Moiselle hugged his shoulder. "I think it bothers you because you know you'd do the same thing that this man did."

He turned to look at her. "You see me like that. That man is a hero. There is no greater love than a man laying down his life for another."

"You're my hero. How about a woman laying her life down for the one she loves?" she said, wanting to kiss him but embarrassed by the gawking white people milling about the plaza. She squeezed his hands as they walked back to the hotel. That night, they danced to the open air of the Champs de Mars on their balcony.

In the morning, while Moiselle was in the bath getting ready to go to the carnival, Robert placed a package on the bed. He waited for her to exit the bathroom. He was grinning like a child about to receive a Christmas gift. "Is it for me or for you?" Moiselle asked.

"This is for you, my darling. I had it made for you."

Moiselle took her time undoing the brown wrapping paper. Inside, the pink satin of a long gown shimmered. The sequined bodice and trim glittered in the dawn's light. There was a long cape attached to the high collar of the dress. "Today, you are going to be queen of carnival, my darling," Robert said.

She jumped off the bed and into his arms and gave him the deepest kiss. He carried her to the bed where their bodies showed full evidence of the spirit of carnival.

A few hours later, Moiselle looked at Robert, unable to believe he had orchestrated so much without her knowledge. "When did you buy the cloth? Who had put this together?"

"I asked your aunt and she recommended Pastor Denis' wife. Your aunt said she could be trusted." Robert made quotes in the air with two fingers as he said, "trusted".

Moiselle clarified. "She is talking about essences. Remember what I told you before. You don't give just anybody things that are personal or that have your essence."

"Essence. Are we an extract?" he joked.

The smile left her face and her eyes narrowed. "I'm serious. With your clothes, underwear, nails, hair or anything that is connected to your soul, people can harm you or take away all the goodness that life has prepared for you."

He frowned. "Superstitions. Is that why you stand guard outside every time you put our clothes to dry on the clothes line?"

"Now you're getting it. But where did you get this beautiful cloth?"

"The pastor's wife seems to know many cloth vendors. I gave her one of your dresses and she did it in less than a week."

Moiselle was getting ready to say something when a gentle knock at the door diverted their attention. Robert opened the door and two young maids dressed in white came in. Their heads were wrapped with the same white cotton material as their simple, ankle-length dresses. They could pass for twins with the same wide foreheads and the same dancing eyes. Robert wondered why

Moiselle gave the girls a sour look. Then, he realized maybe she had seen him talking to the women. Robert was tempted to ask if they were twins, when one of the two girls said, "Sir, the manager requested that we come and assist you."

"Yes, did his wife give you anything to bring for me?" Robert inquired.

One girl lifted a bag and the other one said, "Madame sent us to help dress and do the make-up of the carnival queen."

Robert pointed to Moiselle: "There she is." Then he turned to Moiselle, "I'm going to wash the mule and decorate it." He bowed in an exaggerated manner that made her laugh. The two maids put their hands over their mouths to keep from laughing.

Moiselle's mind traveled back to the white lady in the big, beautifully hidden house in the woods outside of Beudet. She imagined this is what that lady must experience every day of her life. The girls scrubbed Moiselle's back, head, and body with pink soap that smelled like camellias. She imagined that she was the lady from the big house. She told herself that this pampering wasn't a one-time thing. She tried to forget that tomorrow she would be a peasant in the garden pulling weeds, a mother changing diapers, a wife wondering if her marriage was strong enough to keep her husband home. But at that moment, she believed that she was a queen. She allowed the two maids to rub her with oil that smelled like nothing she'd ever smelled before. Vanilla? No. Frangipani? The fragrance made her feel expensive. The maids pulled the dress over Moiselle's head, and it fit perfectly. She twirled around in the small mirror. She sat on the edge of the bed as one girl applied powder to her face. "What is that thing you are putting on my eyes?" Moiselle marveled.

"It's eye make-up. Madame brings it all the time from France. Once she gave me a little box with purple and green eye make-up that she didn't want anymore. You see," she pointed to her eyes, "I wear it all the time. The key is to put in a lot, so when you look in the mirror you will think it is too much, but trust me."

When Moiselle stood again to look at herself in the mirror, some-one else was standing there. "Oh, please don't cry, you'll ruin the make-up and you'll look ugly," the rounder of the two maids said. Moiselle ordered the tears back. She thought of Robert's exagger-ated bow from earlier and this made her laugh again. She turned her head to see how the shorter maid had braided the front and side of her hair into a chignon. The braided chignon was adorned with her favorite flowers: Lady of the Night and red hibiscus.

Moiselle decided to show what a good queen she could be, so she handed each maid the loose change she had brought with her to buy some items for Grace, Charlotte, and Aunt Neila. Thank you, Mademoiselle, you are indeed a queen," the two maids praised.

When Robert returned, she was sitting on the edge of the bed. "David, sir, this is my wife. I was telling you about her; she is going to be the queen of carnival today," Robert said to the balding white man who was following him into the hotel room. He had a wide smile and a camera around his neck.

"You are not kidding; she is a beauty."

He started to take pictures of Moiselle, but Robert stopped him. "Please wait, I have one more thing to give her. He pulled a small box from the back of his pocket. Moiselle opened it to find a pair of gold hoop earrings. She put them on and Robert said, "Now, you look perfect."

No sooner were the words out of his mouth than David began to snap pictures. At first the flash blinded Moiselle, but she blinked rapidly to avoid the momentary blindness. When the photo shoot was over, Robert gave her his arm and escorted her down the stairs. At the bottom of the stairs, the mule waited patiently. Moiselle smiled to see that it, too, had a crown of green leaves and red hibiscus. The saddle's fringes were braided with red ribbons.

Three boys, whom Moiselle had seen hanging on the outside of the hotel since the day they arrived, ran towards them as Robert instructed. "You, young man, will hold my wife's dress from this side. Your brother will hold it on the other side. And your cousin here has the most important job: hold her cape in the back. All of you, listen: Don't let anyone come near her or grab her. This is what I am paying you for."

"When and where did you have time to get them new clothes?" Moiselle asked filled with pride at his benevolence.

He lifted Moiselle and gently placed her on the mule. "It's amazing what a little bit of money and very kind hotel staff can do," he said looking up at her, gleaming with pride and joy.

"Robert Donner!" A gaunt man wearing a gray wool vest even though it was at least 80 degrees out ran toward the couple. Robert turned to face the man and a serious look came over him.

"Brother Thomas, where--"

He cut Robert off with an exuberant handshake. "I was just making plans and asking around about how to get to Croix des Bouquet to come see you this morning. Then, standing on my balcony I see you! I said, "Lord, You do work in mysterious ways."

Moiselle wondered if Robert realized he had untied and tied the throat latch of the horse's harness over five times in the five minutes they had stood facing Brother Thomas.

Moiselle shifted her attention to the bands practicing, getting ready for the procession. Brother Thomas kept his eyes down, but once in a while he glanced at Moiselle. She had seen that look before. It was the look a poor child gives at the front of a store where peanut brittle and other delicious candied goods lined shelves. She caught his gaze and smiled but he turned his head and ran his hand through his hair, as if to pull out any ideas he had about her.

Robert finally said, "I don't know if you've heard, but Pa and I parted ways."

"Well, it's funny you should say that. When I arrived last week, after receiving complaints from three of our churches that they haven't received new Bibles in several years, and after receiving an alarming letter from Ms. White explaining that she was abandoned, I went to our headquarters in Savanne Blanc. This is where I found your father. Robert, he looks grave. He couldn't speak to me for more than ten minutes. Then he had to rest. He is lucky to have that step mother of yours, and of course, Ms. White."

Moiselle interpreted Robert's stone-faced look as shock. She wanted to dismount, to wrap her arms around him and kiss him back to life no matter who was watching. She made an effort to slide down, but Robert stopped her. "I'm coming back to talk," he said to Brother Thomas. Brother Thomas said, "How at noon. You and I can have lunch by the pool. I have pressing business to discuss with you." Robert nodded, and kept looking over his shoulder.

The marching bands sounded more unified, like they could see the door to perfection not too far from them. Robert gave her the donkey's reins. As they exited the yard, the mule's hooves produced the melody of progress on the shiny cobbled walkway. People were coming out of their hotel rooms and applauding. The clicking of cameras was a new kind of music to Moiselle.

They didn't have far to walk to reach the spot where all the carnival bands and participants lined up. Robert had inquired before their arrival and had paid a small entry fee. He didn't know who made the bearded, short, light-skinned man in charge, but everyone deferred to him as Mr. Charlier. "Yes, Mr. Donner, she is a queen. Some of the bands have already lined up, but we will put her at the front. Follow me."

As Mr. Charlier pranced, his ascot, the perfect contrast to his teal chiffon shirt, led the way. He addressed everyone who crossed path with him: "No, no, that sign won't do—too vulgar," he said to one man; "Hey, young man, this is not a rooster fight, go home and get a proper shirt," he said to a boy on the sidelines. "Oh, what is to become of Haiti with these unsociables?"

Moiselle was relieved to see a smile on Robert's face, but wondered if it was just to keep her from asking questions. She wished they could go back to the hotel so he could tell her about this man, and she didn't like that sad look that came over his face every time the man had mentioned his father or Lily White.

Moiselle marveled at all the bands and floats. Suddenly, she saw visions of Grace and thought about how she would enjoy the colors. She could see her fat chubby fingers reaching for the balloons and colorful flags. From looking at the color coordinated bands, it was clear that Robert had done his research. The color of her dress matched the band shirts. Even the float with the jungle theme had pink and white signs.

The first band to open the ceremonies was a new band, *Septentrionale*. The music oozing from their saxophones and their drums was a marriage of what Moiselle had heard at voodoo ceremonies and the merengue her father liked to listen to. The sweet percussion grabbed her heart and twirled it around. She grabbed tufts of the mule's mane to steady herself.

After the opening song, the bands and floats moved like turtles. Moiselle sat regally, swaying on the mule while she waved to the crowd as Mr. Charlier had instructed her to do. Little boys and girls lined up on the side were yelling, "You are the most beautiful queen!" Robert looked at her occasionally and mouthed, "Are you tired?" but she just smiled back and kept waving.

At the juncture of Grand Fort road, the crowd grew increasingly agitated. They pushed towards the area of the band line. The guides stopped the mule as six young men pushed their way into the parade in front of her and performed a choreographed number. Judging by the fluidness and mastery of the syncopation, she knew they had practiced for a long time and had not had the entry fee. This was their only chance to crash the festivities. The crowd mimicked their high intensity dance. Moiselle was mesmerized by their leaps and twirls in the air. "Get out of here right now," an out-of-breath Mr. Charlier, riding on a gray horse decorated with the fuchsia and green of his ascot. He had a machete and he twirled it in the air. His companions, also on mules and horses, tried to push the crowd back so that the queen could move. Robert blocked a few who tried to grab for Moiselle. The path opened up and the crowd was behind the lines once again. As they proceeded, someone hurled a rock. It hit Robert on the head. He fell.

"Robert!" Moiselle yelled, but her screams were inaudible as her three young foot-guards, following Robert's strict orders, continued to propel the mule forward. She tried to get off the mule. "No, Madame, stay on the mule," the young men emphasized, as they pulled her back up. "That's my husband. He is lying down on the road. No let go of me," she smacked their hands and she kicked. Her punt jarred the mule and made him take off faster as he brayed. Looking back as much as she was able to, Moiselle saw a small group gather around Robert to remove him from the road.

Her tears coupled with the eye make-up created a striated pattern on the bodice of her dress. She watched Robert, who was being carried away, grow smaller and smaller. Suddenly, the day felt like it would never end. The mule took twenty thousand and eighty-five steps from the time she and Robert were separated until the time the mule was guided back to the hotel. Moiselle's shoulders slumped, she imagined powerful hands holding the sun and rewinding it, so that the night she needed to end the tiresome day had finally come. The three boys guided her back to the hotel. She jumped off and ran to the lobby. She recognized the manager and he chased after her.

"Mrs. Donner, your husband is okay. Please don't run," he said, panting as he tried to keep up with Moiselle whose legs covered three stairs at a time. "This is the key, let me let you in."

Moiselle allowed him to open the door, holding back the tears. "Where is he?" She patted the bed, ran to the balcony, and even dropped to look under the bed. Mr. Castre struck a match and lit the yellow candles spread out throughout the room in delicate bronze candle holders.

"They bandaged his cut very well. He said you are going to go home tomorrow morning, so he settled the accounts until tomorrow at 10 in the morning. If you need the room for longer let me know." He turned to leave and then hesitated, "I'm sorry, Mrs.

Donner, I almost forgot to give you this." He handed her a sealed white envelope and closed the door behind him.

Moiselle thank you was barely audible. She sat on the bed and read the letter. It was three sentences long.

My anchor, I am not hurt.

She stopped reading the first line and kicked at the bed. She winced and cried as her toe throbbed. When her toe ache subsided, she read the second sentence.

I have decided to go take care of the Bibles and to accompany Brother Thomas, who is going to go see my father. I will return before you miss me.

She wanted to fling something—break up the room, but realized she would be thrown out. She settled for squeezing and screaming through the pillow.

Moiselle curled herself on the bed. She felt completely exposed. On some nearby balcony another hotel guest played the guitar. It slowed the beating of her heart enough to let sleep, but sleep took her back to the start of the carnival line where Robert was leading her, his smile beaming.

"You could have killed him," Eveline said as the circle of elder Cocottes looked upon Surette disapprovingly. "Your job was to follow them and find out where the target is. Moiselle's husband was not the target."

Mireille, another long-limbed, thin girl, stepped out from the shadow of the hut's walls. "We followed him to the hotel and saw him leave with another man. We know we didn't kill him."

Piti motioned for the two girls to approach the circle where the older women sat. "Did anybody see you fling that rock?"

"No, we were like vapor—in and out," Mireille affirmed.

Surette piped in, "They took a car and we tried to follow on our mule and got separated in Tabarre. They went in the direction of Bon Repos and we followed, but it's like they vanished into thin air."

Eveline turned to the young women and said, "You need to go say your goodbyes to your family and loved ones tonight. No contact with any men. Get ready for your surgery." Mireille and Surette didn't move despite the sternness of their directives. Eveline wondered if they heard her. "The other eight in your unit have already had their surgery. We were waiting for you to return. What? Don't tell me you're having second thoughts?"

"It's not that," Mireille said sheepishly, fondling one of her soft braids. "We just want to make sure that when we are finished with our five years of service in the front line, we'll be unsewn?"

Poupette stepped in between the two girls. She extended a warm hand. "When the elders offered me the choice to sew-in I was worried about scaring. Truth be told, I didn't believe that anything could happen to me. I didn't believe that I could be captured and raped." She lifted her skirt, "These scars on my feet and legs are one of many deep scars Colvin Donner left on me."

Surette puked. Quietly, Poupette put down her skirt.

Eveline touched the girls on their shoulders. "You're being deployed to the North to train and to cross over to the Dominican Republic. Let's get ready."

Moiselle returned to Croix des Bouquets without Robert. As she was leaving, David, the photographer, handed her a small picture he had developed. He took her address to keep in touch and mail the others.

She didn't look at the picture until she had been home a whole day. In the picture, she was sitting on the decorated mule, at the gate of the hotel, looking down at Robert and he was looking up at her. Though it was in black and white, she remembered the copper redness of the mule. There was a soft yellowness of the sun.

After she held her plump baby for hours, and cried for most part of the day, she moped around wondering what Robert was doing. Aunt Neila, Papa Boss, and their kids arrived at her door.

"We thought you would stop to see us before coming home," Aunt Neila chastised as Moiselle served everyone lemonade on the porch. It was already too hot to sit indoors. When they asked about Robert, she said, "He stayed to preach. Be back soon, but look what this American man gave me," she said, diverting them to a new topic.

"Is that you, Moiselle?"

"Neila, look at how beautiful your niece is. Robert looks so proud in this picture."

"He organized everything. He hired two maids to help me dress. He even had three boys to carry my cape. You see, look in that corner of the picture. That's two of the boys right there."

"Oh, I see," Papa boss said, squinting. They looked at those pictures and talked for hours. Just as Moiselle hoped, no one questioned Robert's absence after seeing those pictures.

Seeing something new in that picture every day made the three months Robert spent away bearable. She didn't shy away from the chores that Robert ordinarily took care of. She was in the garden, planting new corn when the gate opened. She looked up to see Robert standing by the gate. She didn't say anything and continued to work.

"Silent treatment after not seeing me for three months. Very predictable, Moiselle," he said. He fumed and went to the house. She continued to do her chores and to ignore him. Later she put the dinner on the table and he sat to eat. She ate through the blessing, which she knew irritated him. He talked and played with Grace, who was hanging around her father as if he were a raft on a sinking ship.

After dinner, he read the Bible and they didn't speak. When it was time for bed, she retrieved the straw mat that she had used two years before when she first lived with her aunt and uncle. She was almost asleep when Robert lifted her off the floor and placed her on the bed.

"You sleep on the bed. I'll sleep on the floor," he said, waiting for a response, but she looked at him blankly. "Moiselle, why is it always all or nothing with you?" He leaned into her on the bed, but she didn't move. His face only centimeters from hers he whispered, "When that rock hit my head and we got separated, a few people helped me back to the hotel. The hotel manager called one of the doctors staying there and he helped me. While I laid in bed waiting for you for two hours, I realized that the rock was my whale. Don't you see, like Jonah, I have been going down the wrong way? Once I realized that I got up and resumed my work. Moiselle, I can't stop my work. I'm going to leave again and again. But I will always come back to you. You and our children." He touched the little mound that showed that she was entering her second trimester. She pulled him down onto her and kissed him.

The next time Robert left, he didn't take clothes. Like before, he felt it was easier to leave without telling Moiselle than risk a fit from her. He was gone for two weeks and returned with gifts that made her forget. So, by their third year of marriage, right about the time the crusade came back to town, precocious little Grace got a sister. They named her Esther 4:14 because Robert wanted everyone to know it was God's destiny to be Moiselle's husband and father of her children. Moiselle thought the name to be unusual, but the inventiveness of the name gave Robert such happiness that she didn't fight him.

Esther 4:14 was a beauty, and surely such a beauty will be put to great purpose, he thought. No one could pass her without sucking in his or her breath. Her skin reminded Robert of milky butterscotch pudding, while Grace's skin had more red undertones. Esther 4:14 had soft, straight hair, and the one thing that always differentiated her from Grace and Robert Junior, who was to be born later, were her Asian eyes. Both Grace and Robert Junior inherited Robert Donner's green eyes. Robert thought her difference was cute and weird, but didn't make much of it. He told himself, forgiveness means forgetting. When Moiselle was asked if she had any Asian ancestors, she looked confused. Naturally, everyone thought it was one of those things that would disappear as the child matured.

Papa Boss's row of pink oleanders in front of his house became an obsession for Robert. He nurtured them and gave them various shapes. Those bushes gave Robert a chance to go over Papa Boss's house to talk to him.

"You know why I love oleanders?" Papa Boss asked, looking at Robert as he sharpened his farming tools.

"The colors and the petals?" Robert guessed.

"No, not really. I love the fact that though they have a tendency to roam and take over, if you put them in rich, dark soil with plenty of sunlight, they will stay and not wander for water."

Boss took a minute and looked at Robert who finally said, "I see." When Papa Boss didn't say more, Robert confided, "Papa Boss, you're a wise man. I want to ask you your honest opinion about something."

"Hmm," Papa Boss hummed while wiping his tools. He motioned for his oldest son, Phillippe, to hand him some water. He offered some to Robert.

Robert took a gulp from the same cup. "I've been thinking about starting a school here so I don't have to travel so much. Besides, pretty soon Grace will have to start her education, then later Esther 4:14. I'm thinking the only free place is the Catholic school. I miss preaching every day. I haven't been able to get away since the baby's been born. Moiselle watches me like a hawk. A school's gonna give me a chance to start something small and build up."

"Well, I can't tell you what to do, but I know a man is not a plant. That sounds like some rich soil to me."

"True," Robert said as his voice broke. He stood on the porch watching the sun tilt back for one last stretch before retreating in the distance. The sound of Boss' blades sharpening against the leather echoed in his ears, breaking down the mounds of emotions anchoring him. Soon Robert realized that all the gardening and all the dreaming about starting a school could not scratch the traveling itch of the missionary-preacher. He hadn't started a church out of respect to Pastor Denis, but a school could be a different thing.

Esther 4:14, whom they had taken to calling Tĕtĕ, was about three months old and Robert hadn't been on the road for almost six months when one day, Moiselle feeling confident that somehow the two kids had anchored Robert to her and their home, she decided to go to the market to sell the peppers and tomatoes that Robert had picked. She took Grace and Tĕtĕ with her, as she always did to assuage any suspicion that she was going to go where she wasn't supposed to. Several hours later, she threw open the door to her house, and announced, "Darling, everything sold at top price!" Robert wasn't in the one-room house, so she went around the back to the garden. She saw that the plants had been watered and thought that he must have gone to visit Papa Boss. But his good, preaching suit was gone. In all the times he had left before, he had never taken that black suit. She didn't like the twisting feeling in the pit of her gut, like someone had taken a mortar to her intestines. There was an increasing storm gathering in her head. With Esther 4:14 on one hip and Grace on the other, she half-walked and half-ran to Papa Boss and Aunt Neila's house.

"Aunt Neila!" She knocked on the door. Her aunt came from the back where she was cooking. "Zel, catch your breath. Breathe." Aunt Neila reached for Tètè and immediately Grace lunged for Aunt Neila in protest. "I love you both, Grace," Aunt Neila coo-ed. Then turned, pointing in the direction of her back yard. "Moiselle, let's go out back where I'm getting dinner ready and Charlotte is playing. Come and help me. If you want, we can eat together tonight."

"That's good, auntie. I'm tired. I was at market in Beudet all morning. It was a good day, but you know how tiring people can be. They want to give you less for your merchandise. They turn it this way and they turn it that way. They go up to another vendor and pretend they're no longer interested in your stuff. All the while they know that I have the best, freshest tomatoes and peppers."

Moiselle didn't like that she couldn't get straight to the point of her visit. She didn't want to be rude, so she talked more about the Beudet market and some vendors who had asked about her aunt. "Child, never mind those hypocrites. You know that's why I've stopped going down there since last year." Moiselle laughed at the face her aunt made when she said, "hypocrites," then asked her aunt, "*Matante* Neila, have you seen Robert?"

"Yes. I heard him earlier, about four hours ago. I was back here plucking the chicken, and I didn't want to present myself in that state to him. He hollered from the porch that he had brought some tomatoes and peppers for us. So, I told him about the position I was in and sent Phillippe to retrieve the basket. Robert said he was surprised I was home and not at market with you." A look of worry crossed over Moiselle's face. She pursed her lips and waited for her aunt to continue. "I told him I hadn't seen you that morning and reminded him that the big market day was tomorrow, not today. So now that I know you went to the Beudet market, I understand his confusion." Both women were silent and in their thoughts. Then Aunt Neila said, "Poor Phillippe has been home with a stomach bug. By the way, thank you. Those tomatoes are delicious. You're going to taste them for sure in this meal."

"Are you giving Phillippe *associ*?" Her aunt nodded in acquiescence. "Did Robert tell you where he was going?"

"No, after Phillippe went up front to retrieve the tomatoes and peppers, Robert yelled back to me 'Good-bye *Matante*'."

"Where's Phillippe, *Matante*? Maybe Robert told him something. I don't know where he is. His good suit was not hanging on the nail on the back wall, as it usually is. He has never done that before."

"Calm yourself down!" her aunt said as she held one of Moiselle's arms. "Phillippe is with his father on the farm. You know Boss doesn't get back here until the sun is almost ready to set. Come, help me finish dinner and Boss will be here in another hour."

"Auntie, I can't wait. I'm leaving the girls here with you and I'm going to see Papa Boss." Moiselle sped across the greater part of Rue Stenio Vincent and down the long gravel road to Boss' farm like a gazelle of the spirit world, one of the gods she was silently praying to.

"Phillippe, Phillippe!" She hurled herself at the young boy's knees. "Did Robert, my husband, tell you where he was going?"

Phillippe shook his head, his eyes the size of two quarters wobbling in his head. Papa Boss lifted her off the ground and looked at her tenderly. "Moiselle, I saw Robert walking towards Beudet and Thomazeau about four and half hours ago. He had his suitcase and was trying to hitch a ride."

"No, please say that is not true. Why didn't you stop him, uncle? How am I going to manage three children?" she said touching her belly. She continued, "Woy, woy, Why didn't you stop him, uncle?"

She dashed away from him before he could answer her question. She ran in the direction of Bon Repos.

Someone always sees something on the road in Haiti. Tracking Robert was easy. All she had to ask was, "Did you see a white man carrying a suitcase?" People were so helpful. Most pointed straight forward and said, "That way." However, one toothless old man guiding an oxcart loaded down by dried tobacco leaves pointed out a different road he had seen Robert on less than an hour before. She thanked him eagerly and with the renewed energy of a hunter who has spotted the blood of her injured prey, she forged on.

When she thought the trail was dead and she wanted to return to Croix des Bouquets, she came across four women by the stream, beating their clothes with rocks, making every thread cry out for cleanliness. They worked in unison, singing. Moiselle sat by the river's bank and waited for them to finish their song. She asked the shortest one who happened to be closest to the edge of the river, "Did a white man carrying a suitcase come through here?"

"The white man crossed the stream. He told us he wanted to verify that he was going the right way. Apparently, he hadn't been here since about nine months ago when they put in this gravel road and bridge. I guess it threw him off. He couldn't figure out the path to the Church of the Reverent. We told him to go beyond the plantain farm, and when he saw the ten goats tied to a fence he should go down that road. That's where the church is."

Moiselle washed her face and soaked her aching feet in the river as the sun was going down. Then, she said goodbye to the laundry women and headed for the Church of the Reverent. Their directions were perfect. She passed the plantain field, the ten grazing goats, and went down a small road to find the small white church squatting in the middle of a large meadow.

She looked through the slats of the closed shutter and saw that the church was empty. She walked around the back and saw another small house. This little house looked like her house, except it was white and she thought the four doors indicated four additional rooms. It had the same A-frame construction with the galvanized roof as her little blue house. Its wide porch was painted. There were six chairs exactly like the three chairs that were on her porch. The shutters were accented green instead of blue. The side garden was in a similar position. She walked through the small gate to the garden. Laughter of a family at the dinner table drew her to peek into the small window. Robert's father and step mother were speaking quietly to each other. "How many Bibles were you able to get and distribute?" a woman asked as Robert passed her the bread in a basket. Moiselle shifted to the left and got a full, clear view of blonde cascading curls and the face of Ms. Lily White.

Robert didn't think that after almost two years the dogs would recognize him, but they did. They met him by the half-mile gate of the property of the Church of the Reverent. He walked with them. They licked his outstretched palm. The one with the brown coat and long fox-like face must be Marbles, Robert thought. He smiled as they howled at other dogs in the neighborhood. It reminded him of the sounds he had heard on his journey here, like mermaids calling sailors. A hollow sound that seemed like cries until it hit your ears and then you heard your name clearly. He convinced himself that it couldn't have been his name being called so many times on his way.

"Oh, Lord, this is indeed a joyful day!" Robert's stepmother exclaimed from the porch as he approached the house. Her thick-heeled shoe dragged sound out of the painted floorboards. Robert removed his hat and bowed, "Ma'am, it's good to be back home."

"Don't you ma'am me. I'm but ten years your senior. How many times must I ask you to call me Beverly."

"Thank you, Beverly," he said awkwardly when Lily appeared, wiping her hands on her apron. She stood next to Beverly, smiling. Robert wondered what he should say. The last time they saw each other, they had just met and learned of their betrothal, and then he told her he was leaving to go preach. He wondered if his father and step-mother had told Lily about Moiselle. He decided not to say anything about what he had been doing. "You looking mighty well, Ms Lily," he said, knowing he was being more formal than necessary.

"Come in, Robert. Huguette, Mr. Robert has come home. Fetch him some water to wash the travels off of his hands and face." It wasn't five minutes when a rotund woman with a pretty gap-toothed smile entered the room. She was new, Robert noted. She poured warm water for Robert to wash his hands and face and handed him a towel.

"The prodigal son has returns," Colvin said with so much dramatic flair that even the women laughed. "I'm your only son," Robert said, relieved by the lightness of the moment. The last time he had come with Brother Thomas and his father was cordial. They hadn't stayed long. Now, he thought his father would be angry and not speak to him, but he appeared so thankful that the show-down he expected would not come to fruition. The men shook hands and hugged and slapped each other on the back.

"So, son, how many souls have you brought to the Lord?" Colvin asked.

"Only the Lord knows."

"Oh, you don't have to tell me. I know all too well how these savages pretend to accept the spirit and then the next day, its business as usually—drinking and fucking like rabbits."

"Colvin! We are still ladies in your presence."

"It's the truth, ain't it?" he said, nudging Robert with his elbow. Huguette plopped a steaming bowl of red rice on the table and Robert wondered if the silence was because they realized Huguette had heard. As the sun hung low in the sky and Huguette was laying the food for dinner, Robert felt a coldness come over him. He thought he saw and later he would convince himself that he had not seen a shadow, the shape, the face of Moiselle standing on the outside, watching them as they ate and talked. Already I am seeing her, Robert thought.

A few hours after dinner, Robert was escorted to his room. "This wasn't here last time I was here," he said to his Beverly. "Well, your father added these four rooms. Paid handsomely to do it, too. He sure complains about it any chance he gets," she said as she fluffed his pillow. "There should be a chamber pot under your bed. If there isn't, call Huguette and she'll get you one." Beverly gave Robert a half smile and left.

Robert didn't realize how tired he was until he dropped onto the bed—fully clothed. Instantly, sleep overtook him. In the middle of the night, it was the tightness of his penis that woke him up. It stood up, wanting to burst out of his pants like a rod searching and looking to reveal water. Clumsily, eyes filled with sleep, he tried to find the chamber pot. It was too late to call Huguette and besides, he didn't even know which room was hers. He decided to look. Three kerosene lamps hung on small shelves in the hall, illuminating the hallway. Still, he took the one in his room, so he could have more light. He knew the door to the right of his was his fathers because he had gone in there while Beverly inspected Robert's room. Slowly, he opened the door across from him and saw that it was a depot where church items were stored. He stumbled down the hall and while standing outside of the one door he heard faint moans. Gingerly, he opened the door. Someone was above his stepmother and the look on her face as pleasure overtook her made him cringe. When he heard, "Robert. Son, you need the outhouse?" from behind him, he turned abruptly and rushed past his father and into the night air, not caring of any danger, just wanting to get away.

Robert Junior, called Bobby, was born after Mango season, six months after his father took his good suit and left home. Aunt Neila visited every morning before her husband left for the farm. She moved through the dew like a leaf dancing in the wind. "I ran over here to make sure the kids had something to eat. Moiselle, you must get out of bed," she cajoled.

"Matante, I get up and I take care of my children."

"You're not the same. Something happened that day when you left those girls with me and ran after Robert, what happened?"

"I found the Church of the Reverent and saw the light."

"Here you go again, speaking in riddles. Okay. I'm going to give you a break today. I'm taking Grace and Tété. See if you can clean up and do some laundry."

A few months progressed and no one, not five-year-old Grace, nor two-year old Esther 4:14, and certainly not the newborn, realized how much Robert's absence affected Moiselle. It tore into her, and this is when the night knocks started.

The first night a man came to knock on Moiselle's door, he brought tafia.

"Samson, what are you doing here so late?" she asked, looking at him from his beat up work boots to his dirty straw hat.

"I haven't seen you at the bar for a week, so I thought you might be sick. I don't have to come in. You need company?" There was an un-zippering effect to his plea and loneliness that matched hers. She opened the door to him and found that she wasn't taking another man to her bed, but old business, unfinished past.

The next morning, Moiselle got up and staggered outside of her house. "Grace, is that you? What are you banging and against what?" she mumbled. Grace was hitting a stick against the thin wooden post that held the porch's roof.

"Manman, look!" she said, pointing her finger at the window. Moiselle's screams flowed seamlessly like a song, out of her mouth. There was no time for thoughts or breaths. It was her soul pouring out of her body, escaping the confines of her flesh, being loose on the world. She stared at the red paint of her window sill. When her throat was too raw to emit sound, she grabbed buckets of water and a rag and tried to rub the paint off of her windows, but it didn't come off.

Hours later, Aunt Neila said, "Moiselle, give me this rags; "You're scrubbing your skin off. That's your blood on the rag, not paint."
****

Pastor Daniel Denis sat at the Donner's dinner table, smiling at the numerous plates that Huguette plopped in front of him. He had complimented Beverly on making such a small house look so very beautiful. He had done a lot of short talk and wanted to get to the point, but Colvin Donner interjected with glee, "Beverly, this guy is something else. Did I ever tell you about the time we went old testament." Pastor Denis waved his hands as if to quiet Colvin in a playful manner. In a voice full of laughter, Colvin continued, "We had had a great night of preaching about four years ago. Remember, Daniel about Joshua a Rahab. We decided to paint the windows of the town whores red—just like in the Old Testament." He slapped the table top as both men laughed. Then, Daniel clapped his hands and gave one of his jovial laughs and said, "Pastor Donner, I really don't want to worry my wife tonight. I wasn't intending to stay. I was passing by from visiting with that new denomination and thought I had to stop to see you." Colvin's smile disappeared at Daniel Denis's mention of a new denomination. Colvin's blue eyes narrowed as he heaped mashed breadfruit onto his plate and said, "What do you mean new denomination? Are you thinking of leaving us after all we've done for you?" There was a moment of silence. A moment similar to a plane trying to lift off the ground and one holding one's breath and hoping that it does. Daniel Denis said with a slow assuredness, "Well, it seems like I've heard some things that I find disturbing. More disturbing than what I've heard is what I've seen. Right now, my mind is on my wife." He looked at Colvin who looked like his skin was coated with snow. Beverly and Lily who were staring at each other, swallowing very slowly, were about the same shade. Robert, who had grown a beard and a halo of soft blond curls surrounding his flushed face, didn't look up at Denis until he said, "A man should never abandon his wife. As you know, the good book is clear. A man leaves his mother and father and must join his wife. The good book says that." He shook his head as he sucked food items stuck between his top teeth. Robert's was fixed on to Pastor Denis who continued to enunciate, "And those beautiful innocent creatures left alone can do unimaginable things." He paused to look Robert's way. Robert lowered his eyes. Denis continued, "Recently, I learned about one poor, sweet, beautiful girl from my town who married a blan and for whatever reason, he abandoned her. Well now her windows are painted red, so even in the deep of night, other vile men know this is where they can go to satisfy themselves."

Robert nearly choked on his food and began to cough. He managed, in between bouts of cough, to say, "Excuse me." He left the table.

In his room, he cried in his pillow. He didn't know when Pastor Denis left. He was relieved that neither his father nor Beverly, whom he was sure also understood the story, had come to talk to him. Would his father be happy about the outcome? He could just picture him saying, "I told you to stay away from those black witches."

Robert fell asleep, but was awakened in the middle of the night by Huguette's soft, warm hands running over his body. It was their Saturday night routine it seemed. He was always so ashamed, but grateful to be able to have all of Sunday morning to atone after such a night of succumbing to her touch, but tonight there was something in him that wanted to destroy the world. If he was honest with himself, he would see that he wanted to destroy Moiselle. He was surprised that she didn't sense this anger breeding inside of him. Didn't he look harangued with his hair tousled and eyes red from crying? How could she not sense it?

Suddenly, he grabbed her at the waist. She moaned—a cue out of their foreplay repertoire. She opened her arms for him to enter, but he turned her around—away from his face—as if arresting her. He placed her on all fours and mounted her as if she were a bitch. He didn't hear her wince. He didn't care that he was pulling on her arm, her hair, her flesh, screaming hateful insults.
****

As days lined up like bread crumbs, leading her away from the memories of the Church of the Reverent, she had trained Grace to take Esther 4:14 and Bobby to the front veranda where often they fell asleep huddled together on the sleeping mat, as she took care of her male companions.

Come rara season, it was common to find Moiselle barricaded in her house so that she did not hear the calling of the passing rara drums. Instead, she moved only to the rhythm of those nighttime knocks.

One day, a man knocked on the door. He didn't go in as the children went to sit on the veranda.

"Can I help you?" Moiselle asked at the door.

"Don't pretend you don't know me Moiselle." He pulled out a bottle of five star Barbancourt from his straw bag. Her eyes widened and delighted. "I see you remember the finer things in life," he mused.

"So, what Jean-Pierre," she said, still remembering his finger digging into her forehead the night he told her about Lily White a few years back.

"I was looking at this bottle of rum the priest gave me and remembering how Samson was telling the guys how much fun he and you were having drinking, I thought we could share a drink for old time sake."

Moiselle stared at him for a long time. Finally, she took the bottle from him. "Come on in. Don't be coming around here every night," she opened the door for him. But he did come around every night.

One night, as he passed the children on the porch, he bent on one knee and said, "Grace, right? I think it's your birthday today. Look what I have for you." It was a doll made of brown cloth. Grace didn't own a doll and didn't know what to do with it, but she touched the pink satin dress on the doll.

"What do you say?" her mother admonished.

"Thank you, sir."

"Call me Jean-Pierre, Uncle Jean-Pierre. If you are a good girl, I will bring my guitar and one day, I will play for you, your sister, and brother. How does that sound?" Moiselle watched the blank look on Grace's face; so she just shook her head up and down. She called him uncle when he visited every week—sometimes three times a week.

*****

"Robert, your father is outside dancing in the rain," Huguette screamed from the doorway, not entering his bedroom. Robert acknowledged her message, but the sharp rigid way in which she held her wide body at the door gave him another message. He knew she was telling him through her body language that the raw way he had grabbed her, pulled her into this very room, and placed her on all fours and mounted her as if she were a bitch, was never going to happen again. He felt sickened by that memory. When had he become a man driven by raw needs? A man who took, he wondered.

He dropped his pen and the Bible from which he was reading fell to the floor, as silently as it had stared back at him all these years since he had left Moiselle. He used his second eye, the one he had grown since he left Moiselle. The second set of eyes were in the same place as his regular eyes, but he knew now how to make them come out. Like the lens of an alligator that allows the animal to see through water, this second set of lenses helped him not run like an animal as he had the urge to. For example, now, through those lenses he didn't see the rounded mounds of Huguette's ass that reminded him so much of Moiselle. He saw only the long hall of the house and heard the creaking front door and the thundering rain. He halted behind Huguette, who was pointing to the Mapou tree in the distance where his father was shouting at the sky and the tree. "Champagne, I'm ready. Bring the thunder. Didn't you say you would and could bring the thunder? Didn't you say our fate was sealed? Where are you?"

A series of shrill yelps caught his attention. "Beverly, what's going on?" Robert demanded, turning left to look at his yelping stepmother. "I didn't think he would run out that far. I promise. I only took him to stand here for some fresh air," she said, the tears lingered in her eyes for a long time before falling slowly down her cheek. "I bet you did," Robert said dryly, his fingers digging into the fleshy part of her arm, as he remembered his first night in this house. How he had stumbled out of bed, his body aching for Moiselle, his penis a rod leading him outside for relief. He passed his stepmother's bedroom and as he heard moaning, he saw that the two people in the bed were not his stepmother and father, but his stepmother and Lily White. The memory made him want to squeeze her neck.

A drenched Lily approached them. "He won't come away from that tree," Lily said through trembling, blue lips. "I'll go get him," Robert said, not looking at Lily. Since that night when he found out about the two women's affection for each other, he had never looked at Lily in the eyes again. "We'll talk more about this later," he snapped at his stepmother, then he ran toward the towering tree under which his father stood, gesticulating and dancing to some music only in his head. Suddenly, lightening snaked through the sky. Robert ran towards him, but before Robert could reach him, Colvin had been knocked down by a branch of the tree struck by lightning. Robert shuddered at how close the lightning came to hitting his father.

Three nights after the lightning incident, Robert stood at the foot of the bare pine bed, grateful that darkness filled every crevice of the room. Still his father laid like a bloated pig on the bed. His skin glowed in the darkness and the sheet could not mask the heaps of distended flesh under. Robert approached him to see if he were breathing, but inhaled the putrid smell of his father's decaying flesh and gagged. He fell to the ground in a coughing fit. When he gained his composure, the look of terror on his father's face told him all. His father understood that he smelled worse than an outhouse.

His stepmother and Lily White each flanked the wooden bed, singing hymns. Robert wished he could end their hypocrisy by throwing them out, but he knew he couldn't handle his father and manage the congregation without their help. But still, he thought, I need to come up with a plan. Despite himself, he half-listened to the women's discordant tune. Lily had a low, off-pitch singing voice that was slightly muffled by the handkerchief fastened around her face. Even the white makeshift nose mask couldn't improve Beverly's chirps. The acrimonious singing was proof to Robert that his father had indeed gone deaf. The most vibrant thing in the room was the frail flame dancing in the hand-blown glass, hurricane table lamp. The pink and purple floral motif at the brass-finished base casted shadows of creatures. Robert thought that Grace would name that one donkey, and that one she would see a bird and make stories about the animals; Tete would mimic and mumble every word that Grace said, he thought. Maybe Tete would be speaking on her own now. He shook his head, but of course like the other thousand times that day, thoughts of Moiselle, Grace and Tete returned and rested on his shoulder like a pesky pet. In a few weeks, he would have spent six Easters away from them.

Colvin Donner raised two fat fingers, signaling Robert to come near. Robert approached and placed his ears near his father's mouth, careful not to make the same mistake he had made earlier when he breathed in.

"Don't let me die without my rope," he said through labored breath. Robert remembered where he had buried it. It wasn't easy going back to face Moiselle, but he would have to one of these days. He looked at Lily and Beverly and didn't trust the care of his father to them. He found Huguette in the kitchen. "Can I have a word with you, please?" She hesitated. "No, it's not for that. I'm sorry for what it was. You deserved gentleness and I was wrong." She didn't say anything.

In the dim Kerosene lit room, he could see her better. For the first time he noticed the cross on her left shoulder. His father had told him when he was young, it was the mark of the saved. "I see that you're a believer, Huguette and I need to leave the next day to go retrieve an item very precious to my father. I want to trust his well-being to you." She continued to wipe dishes and said, "Sure, don't I take care of him every day?"

Robert smiled, "Yes, but I just don't want another episode like what happened three days ago to happen to him. Huguette smiled back and said, "Not a problem, Mr. Robert." Robert packed a few things to leave Bon Repos.

That very night in Croix des Bouquets, Moiselle had fallen asleep as Jean-Pierre was satisfying himself.

He woke her up. "Damn it, why is it that only your body is here, where is you damn mind?" Her slurred speech showed more than her sleepy eyes how much she had had to drink. "My mind and heart don't belong to me," she mumbled. He laughed, removing himself from between her legs. "You're so fucked up in the head. Do you think Robert is even thinking about you? Do you think he's making himself so drunk that he doesn't know when someone is fucking his brains out?" She started to laugh but then she whimpered, "I miss him so much. He loves me, you know. I'm his anchor."

"Whatever that means. I bet you don't even know that his father killed his mother. Oh, don't look surprised. Didn't he tell you that? That secretive mother fucker." Moiselle rose up with quickness. She kneeled on the bed meeting him eye to eye. "You're mean and you're lying, Jean-Pierre. His mom drowned when their town flooded." Jean-Pierre jumped off the bed, laughing. "That's what he told you?" The more her eyes widened, the more he laughed. Finally he said, "Well, maybe it was a month after they first came to town. Robert was out roaming town—who knows where he was. Maybe he was with you by the river or cemetery. His father asked me to get him some moonshine. I did. White man can't handle that shit. He turned so red. And was throwing stuff around. Then, one of the maids and I helped him to his room—you do know that he and his wife don't share a room, right? Okay, well, we put him in the bed. I was looking through some of his things when all of a sudden, with quickness, he got out of bed and out of nowhere he was using this rope like a whip. He snagged a young maid who was tidying up before we were to leave. He held the rope around her neck. Everyone was rushing to get her out. Here is this fool talking about, 'You love Benjamin more than me, Violet? How could you fuck that nigger? Did Robert see you fuck him, Violet?' Meanwhile, the poor young maid is going limp. He had managed to drag her out of his room and into the yard. I jumped over the half wall that separated him and us—the people who had heard the yelling had gathered. I knocked him over the head with the moonshine bottle. Here comes Robert just after I had done it. 'Jean-Pierre, you're an ass. How could you hit an old man over the head?' He administered to his father who is rumbling, 'Benjamin, you stay away from my Violet or I swear to God I'll lynch you myself.'"

Jean-Pierre ended the story. Moiselle got off the bed and walked towards the decanter and washing pail. Jean-Pierre had caught her attention the moment he mentioned Benjamin, the man Robert said was like a father to him when Colvin Donner was binge drinking. *How did he know the real name of Robert's mother, Violet?* She turned cold and then hot. "You're a sorry son of a whore," she said. She stood by her door, the peignoir revealing the soft bump of her belly and a tuft of soft curls below. As he put on his clothes, he said, "I'm not the son of a whore; I just like to fuck whores." As he left, he stopped at the door and looked at her. "What a waste."

She spat on his face. "I won't be wasting any more time with you. Don't come around here no more."
****

Six women galloped into the yard of the Church of the Reverent. Their wide brim straw hats covered their faces, and long green skirts covered their weapons. Huguette rushed outside and met them. "Welcome, elders," she said.

"Anyone here?" Poupette asked, untying the hat as she entered the house. The other women followed as Huguette explained, "The son left at dawn, and fifteen minutes later the two women went the opposite way. They made plans to go south to Okay to catch a boat back to America."

Colvin hadn't received the opium that Robert had given Huguette to administer for his pain. He was moaning and vomit leaked out of his mouth. The room smelled like an outhouse.

"Oh, you recognized me don't you?" Poupette leaned in as his eyes grew. She paced beside the pine bed. She touched the walls and everything. The other five women looked on, the crosses on their noses gleaming with sweat. "Open the windows, Huguette, please," Poupette asked as she turned toward the swollen Colvin. Colvin laughed and sounded like the sputtering of an old car. Like no amount of air was enough to fill his lungs. "Me Wings" he chortled. Poupette spoke to Colvin from the footboard, "Your son told you about my daughter." He continued his coughing laugh and said, "I see the mango tree too." The words triggered something inside of Poupette. Her hands shook as she slapped him across the face. She said, "Your son may have told you about my daughter's dream, but it is only a dream. You will never leave to see a hair harmed on her head. You're literally rotting. For the past year, I've had my girl here poison you in small doses. I've been buying time." The other women shook their heads; no one interrupted her. This was her moment. Poupette continued, "Part of me wants to make sure you suffer forever. I could watch you rot away right here. And part of me just doesn't want to give you another minute in this world—even if it is a miserable minute. Before four in the morning, I got the message that you would be here alone. I came to make sure the last face you saw was mine." She pulled out a machete. The edge glistened. She cut him from his neck down to his pelvis. He gurgled blood as gas escaped his innards. The other women hastily sprayed the bed with kerosene. Poupette lit the match and threw it on the bed. She didn't look back. Seven birds flew out of the house. The six horses followed. In the distance, neighbors looked in awe to see such big, beautiful birds and the thundering horses that followed their every turn.

By this time Grace was eight; Moiselle didn't leave her house any more. Instead allowing Grace to go to the free missionary school, she sent her to market with a basket of goodies to sell. "Walk your sister to the free school. You can eat if they offer you. Don't stay to play or pay. Go straight to the market. Do you hear me?" Grace kept her eyes down, showing respect as "uncle" Jean-Pierre had told her to. It has been a few days since she had seen him. He has never stayed away that long before. Grace wondered if he would ever come back. Her mom lifted her chin and looked her in the eyes. "In this basket are peppers, tomatoes, and carrots. Find your grandmother and sit next to her. She will make sure no one cheats you. Don't look at me like that. You're not a baby, you're eight years old," Moiselle said, running her hand through Grace's curly afro.

Moiselle stayed home to cook, clean, wash and took care of those men bold enough to come knocking during the day. One day, she came to the door to answer a soft knock. Her face changed when she saw her aunt leaning on the decrepit railing.

"I didn't come to fight, Zel. Only to tell you that you are flapping too high. People are talking."

"Let them talk, Auntie," she said, her head leaning against her door frame.

"You keep doing what you're doing and you will bring about complete shunning." Her eyes rested on the scarlet window pane.

Moiselle followed her eyes and she said, "I don't care anymore. The color looks good on the house. They can do and say what they want. And if I die today, bury me with the dogs."

"Okay." Aunt Neila pretended to wash her hands and walked towards her house.

After Aunt Neila's tall frame disappeared down the road, she crawled back to bed, lying on her side, looking at the floor. Grace, who pretended to have left for the market got in the bed and kneeled behind her mother. She stated to unbraid her mother's hair. Grace's little fingers rubbed oil in her mother's scalp and she hummed the song that her father and her mother and her used to sing when they would sit in the garden, weeding. It wasn't long before Tete followed suit and started to rub her mother's foot as Grace had shown her to do. Bobby laid on his belly on the floor, sucking his thumb. Tears rolled out of Moiselle's eyes.

The next day was bright and even the wind didn't dare come out, when Grace got home from the market, the door to the house was shut. She knew to keep the kids outside playing quietly on the veranda or in the front yard.

"*Cache cache Lubin!*" Grace called out her favorite hide-and-seek call response game. But instead of Esther 4:14's sweet voice, a deep voice answered: "*Seré lubin.*" She turned around. "Daddy!" Grace screamed. Robert Donner was walking down the dirt road and into the yard. When he reached the porch, he hoisted Esther 4:14 onto his huge chest and kissed her. Bobby, not wanting to be left out, jumped up and down, begging to be lifted up into those big arms.

"Who are you, handsome fellow?"

"That's my brother, Bobby! Who are you?" Esther 4:14 said.

Robert's face became joyous as he tossed Bobby in the air repeating, "I'm your papa!" The children started to sing, "Papa! Papa!" When he was out of breath from tossing the children up in the air, he sat on the first step of the porch. Grace noticed how Bobby favored him. Holding all three kids against him, he asked, "Where's your mother?"

Six-year-old Esther 4:14 said, "Inside with our uncle. Grace said we have to be quiet, and Grace won't let us go inside to eat and I'm hungry."

Robert looked at Grace. "Take your brother and sister to Papa Boss's house and stay there."

"If you want Papa Boss to come here, he won't. Only Aunt Neila comes here. Phillippe told me that Papa Boss won't come here because *manman* is a *Bouzen*. But Phillippe won't tell me what it is and when I asked *manman*, she slapped me."

Robert hugged Grace for a long time. He noticed how dirty the children were. Bobby wore an oversized shirt that probably belonged to a teenage boy and had no underwear on. Esther 4:14 had underwear, but no dress. Grace wore a faded green dress with one spaghetti strap. The four chairs he had built for the front porch were broken and strewn around the yard. There were rolled up sleeping mats on the front porch. The chicken coop had a hole in it. There were only three chickens and they were tied to the dilapidated garden fence post. The side garden had more weeds than plants. The blue paint had worn off the shutters and they looked like the bare wood of shipwrecked boats. The sight of the red painted window sills sliced through him. A sad look crossed Robert's face as he tousled Grace's hair and silently urged her towards Papa Boss' house.

Robert knocked several times and no one opened the door. Then, he kicked the door down. The man inside came running out of the house fixing his shirt, hopping on one leg as he tried to push the other leg into the other pant leg. Robert scrambled after the man with speed and managed to knock him back with a few blows across the face. Then he ran into the house after his Moiselle.

Grace thought her father was going to run to her mother and lift her up and kiss her, as she remembered he used to do. Looking from behind the tree not too far from the house, she saw something different. Robert's palm hit Moiselle's face, and it made a clamor louder than her screams.

"What was I supposed to do? God sends no manna here," Moiselle stammered. This statement got her another slap and she fell back on a crate of empty bottles.

Then, Moiselle stood defiant, her eyes wide with tears.

"I'm sorry," Robert whispered looking at his hand as if it were possessed. He lifted it toward Moiselle. He didn't see or know where she got a knife. He felt the cut across his palm.

"For the love of God, Moiselle," he winced.

"You have no right to put your hand on me. I swear, I will put this through your cold heart if you touch me again," Moiselle said.

Robert ran around the room, looking for a piece of cloth to tie around his cut. Instead he spotted empty bottle after empty bottle of liquor. No wonder the kids have no clothes and look thin--it all goes into the bottles he thought.

He looked at his hand. The cut wasn't deep, but he let the blood fall to see Moiselle's reaction. She stood like a stone lion. He approached her gently with both palms up and a gentle expression on his face.

"You're my wife and you're whoring yourself out."

She turned her back to him, wiping out tears. "I'm not your wife. Do you have papers to prove it?"

Robert opened his mouth to say something, but her cool logic fettered him.

"You're no different than any man who walks through that door. The way I see it is that I spent two years sleeping with you. You left. We have children together. I don't belong to you. I don't have any feelings for you."

"Moiselle, don't say that," he said, hanging his head.

"I'll say and do what I want to do. Six years you've been gone. You don't even know your son. Don't judge me and don't feel sorry for yourself. You did this. The only thing I regret is that I chose you over Ling. You know he came back for me. The night you found us dancing at the bar, he proposed to me again. He wanted to take me to China. I chose you, but you couldn't choose me."

"If I were a soldier and left for war, would you have done what you did? You shake your head to say that it's not the same thing, but you know you wouldn't have whored yourself. You don't respect my work as a soldier of the Lord. I was doing God's work. I have to choose *God*."

"Robert, you chose another woman and your father. Go home to her and your Church of the Reverent."

Robert backed away at the mention of the church's name, which he had never told her. He knew she knew. He didn't want to look into her eyes. He looked up at the rafts. His hands ached remembering how he skinned and shaped the wood of that the one mango tree that was on the property to make the beams to hold the ceiling. Fastened to those rafters was his father's rope—his rope, doing double duty of no doubt a swing for the kids. How did she get it up there? He had hidden that rope under the house's floor board. He didn't think she would find it. How his father has begged for that rope. He hoped he would reach his father in time. He thought of sharing that news with her and then decided not to. There were enough complications between them.

"Go away Robert," Moiselle said, as if she had no more breath left in her body.

He brought his eyes down to her. "Moiselle, one thing always leads to another. I meant to tell you when I first came back that--"

"That you married your white woman on paper, but you made a fool of me in front of my family and my village. Call me a whore if you want, but at least I'm not fooling myself anymore.

Go home. Since you built this house, which is just like your house for your real wife, I can understand you might be confused, but this is not your house." She moved to stand in front of the bedroom section of the one-room house. The half of the house where he stood looked like it had been through a storm. Clothes, dishes, chairs were overturned, items hanging on the wall were covered with cobwebs, including a picture of him and Moiselle at the gate of the Excelsis Deo hotel before they went to the carnival almost seven years before.

The only clean part of the house was where the bed was. Robert recognized the canopy over the bed immediately. It was the cape from Moiselle's carnival queen outfit. The pillows were made from parts of her carnival dress.

"You want to see your children, come around to see them, spend time with them, or take them for a little while. You want me: pay like every other man for five, ten, twenty minutes between my legs." Moiselle's arms were akimbo like the day they met at the well.

Not caring or fearing her knife, Robert ran to her and grabbed her. He kissed her the way he had been dreaming of and wanting to.

She fought him at first, hitting him on the head and shoulder with her fists. Then, fists loosened. She held on to him. His touch came back to her like an old, sweet song. There was a lingering, a savoring. They held each other, not moving, smelling each other to the very core. If souls could touch, theirs would have. Robert's touch sent sensations coursing through her body. He licked her tears. As Moiselle fell into the deepest ecstasy, she thought of love as a formidable opponent. *Even when you're down, love wants more.* With everything in the little house turned over, they made love to each other.

When they were finished, Robert got up and placed five dollars on the table. Not even the thump of the slamming door could muffle the sobs coming out of Moiselle.

The day her father returned after his six-year absence, a scared Grace ran with her siblings to Papa Boss's house. There they slept for the night and wore hand-me-downs from Charlotte and Phillippe. In the late afternoon, Grace picked up Esther 4:14 and Bobby from the *Martenelle* section of the free missionary school. On the walk home, Esther 4:14 had so many questions: "Do you think Papa will stay? Do you think Papa will let me ride on his back like a horse again? That's going to be so much fun." Grace was quiet. She was hoping that her parents had stopped fighting.

When they got home, the door was closed. She knew not to open a closed door, so she and her siblings played outside. She checked the garden. Her mother had told her about times they had spent in the garden. No one was there.

When it was dark and her mother still hadn't turned on the kerosene lamps, Grace tugged at the door. It opened. "Tete, stay with Bobby out here. I think Momma and Papa went out. I've got to turn on the lamps before we can go in."

Tete sat with Bobby on the porch's first step. Inside, Grace stumbled over scattered furniture. After she opened the curtains to let the moonlight in, she saw the lamp still propped on the kitchen table. She struck the match and lit the lamp. When she got to the middle of the room, she froze. She saw her mother's limp body like a faded dress, like a mango the birds have pecked, hanging from the ceiling swinging without direction. Moiselle's eyes bulged out of her head and streaks of blood had caked her bloated face.

It was Tete's screams that finally wrenched Grace's scream from her throat. The siblings following Grace's lead stumbled out of the house in the direction of Papa Boss' house.

Aunt Neila wanted to bury Moiselle behind the little house that Robert had built for them, but Papa Boss suggested that a dead body behind the house might cause complications if they ever wanted to sell the property to help out with the children. Grace didn't understand what was going on. She sat in a corner on the porch. Aunt Neila and her grandmother had not entered the house to see the body Papa Boss had laid on her bed. Grace wondered what they were waiting for. It seemed like everyone in town was lined up outside the dilapidated fence, talking and pointing. Street vendors had set up temporary posts outside the gates.

Then, like a squall, twelve women in white entered the yard. Their white straw hats had white veils that covered their faces and heads. They wore white gloves. They carried a white-washed, wooden casket. The casket had red hearts and a mermaid tail painted in red on each side. The two women in the back were the tallest and it sloped down until it reached the front two who were about four feet tall. Silently, they entered the room, walking backwards. Out from under those dresses came special potions and oils. There was a white cloth. Grace stood in the doorway and watched as the veiled women washed and oiled her mother's body. Then they wrapped her in white cloth and placed her in the wooden casket.

Grace didn't know what to call what she saw. Was it a dream? When the women exited the house, the casket weighing more now, they hummed. Each two holding the casket above her head had a different hum—like different instruments of an orchestra. They walked backwards out of the house. The crowd parted and everyone followed. Grace felt someone grab her hand and she looked up and it was Phillippe. Papa Boss was walking behind with Bobby and Esther 4:14 and his other two children. She jumped up to see if she could see her father in the crowd. Where was her aunt? Where were they going? She counted one hundred steps almost 89 times. She had never been to this place. She liked the colorful houses with the crosses on them. She wanted to take one. She would live there, but someone had put his name on the little house.

One of the white-washed little houses had the same mermaid tail as the coffin. She whispered, "Where are we Phillippe?"

"This is the cemetery. La siren's tomb. Don't you know anything?"

Grace watched as the women fluidly lowered her mother's coffin into the mausoleum. That's when it hit Grace that she was never going to see her mother again, and then when the women hummed, she knew and understood how to begin.

*****

It was agreed that the children were going to be better off in Croix des Bouquet with Papa Boss and Aunt Neila, not in Beudet with their grandparents who, although they lived less than 6 miles away, hardly knew the children.

No one spoke of her mother and father. Grace hated that. She felt like everyone was pretending that nothing had happened. Grace went every day after school to sweep around the crypt. She traced the great big mermaid tail on the tomb. Sometimes she ran through the cemetery screaming her mother's name. Grace wanted everyone to know that she remembered her—even if they didn't.

It was on one of those days when she snuck out of school that she went back to their old house. She went to her mother's bed. This room was sacred. She never went in there except to help dust and clean. The pillow smelled of night jasmine and crushed Lady of the Night flowers. The pillow smelled like her mother. Grace closed her eyes and held the pillow to her chest. It was as if she were holding her mother. She walked to the small window overlooking the garden. There was a picture of her mother and father against the wall. Her mother was on a donkey wearing the most beautiful costume she had ever seen. The flowers around her mother's head made her look like a queen. She took the picture and the pillow.

In the center of the room was the rope. No one had the heart to take it down. She stumbled outside and sorrow came out of her mouth. After she had vomited for the last time, she stood looking at the red painted window. Through the window, it looked like the rope with its scarlet streaks was hanging from the window. She knew it wasn't and went back inside. A chair laid on its side, the cane section of the seat perforated. Grace pushed it to the side. The rope moved when she touched it. It coiled into a ball. She took it down. Grace extended it and tied a knot. Then, she wrapped it around a tree so she could manage to get that knot tight---taut as an angry knuckle.

Grace began to wear that rope around her belly--under her clothes. Aunt Neila expressed concern to her husband: "What is the meaning of this child carrying this rope around; she looks ridiculous. What are we going to do?"

"She's traumatized and only time and patience will help her find her way again," Papa Boss whispered. Grace said nothing. She grew silent.

One day, a month after her mother's burial, Papa Boss saw her standing at the top of the road leading to his property, near the pink oleander bushes. He went to stand next to her. He placed his hands on her shoulder. She looked up at him and said, "One day I'm going to kill my father." The wind whirled around them, but couldn't carry those words away. They were heavy, like a loaded cannon. As Papa Boss walked back toward the house with her, she touched that knot, that first knot on the rope. The first knot is for her mother. The rope wounded tightly around her belly, demanded blood. It cut off any love Grace had in her heart. The rope shifted, like an awakened serpent.

THE END

About the Author

Born in Port-au-Prince, Haiti, and with vivid memories rooted in the Croix des Bouquets arrondissement, MARIE KETSIA THEODORE-PHAREL is a celebrated Haitian author known for her profound storytelling and contributions to Haitian literature. Her extensive experience as a writer and cultural activist lends depth and meaning to her storytelling, immersing young listeners in the world of Haitian folklore and history. Through her expert storytelling and use of dialogue and colorful imagery, she brings her characters and stories to life while also providing insightful commentary on Haiti's past and present. Her work spans a variety of genres, including children's literature and novels, exploring themes deeply entrenched in Haitian culture and history. Theodore-Pharel's engagement with her craft and her dedication to portraying the Haitian experience have made her a significant voice among contemporary Haitian writers.

Ketsia earned a bachelor's from Tufts University and a masters in English from University of Massachusetts, Boston. She was a recipient of the 2017 and 2019 State of Florida Folklife apprenticeship for storytelling. Her notable publications include "Mercy at the Gate" in Haiti Noir, edited by Edwidge Danticat, 2011; "Haiti: a Cigarette Burning at both Ends" in Butterfly Ways: Voices from the Haitian Diaspora in the United States, edited by Edwidge Danticat, 200. Her children's books include Beauty Walks in Nature, Songs from a Tower, Keeper of the Sky, One More Daughter, America, Daughter of the House, A Fish Called Tanga, and I'll Fly Away.